The Holy Writings According to קסת הסופר

הנה אנכי ח"ד בי"ד

שנת התשע"ד
מקום גלותינו
New York

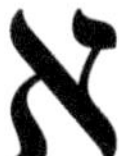

Who is fit to write holy sefer torahs, tefillin and mezuzahs. And to purchase from them.
6 sections

1) תניא Rabbi Meir said, when I came by Rabbi Yishmael he said to me "My son what is your work?" I replied to him "I am a scribe". He said to me: "my son be careful in your work for your work is the work of heaven. Lest you be lacking one letter or have one letter extra and you have destroyed the entire world." It is thus evident that the sofer must fear Hashem to the utmost. For if he made a mistake or he did not do something properly, he forfeits his soul. He has stolen from the public and brought them to sin. For they are left without מצות and they bless each day for naught. Regarding him the verse says וחוטא אחד יאבד טובה הרבה and one sinner can destroy much good. It is also written ארור עושה מלאכת ה' ברמיה cursed be he who does the work of Hashem in trickery. Tto those who have the power is the obligation to appoint proper scribes. Men of honesty who do not take bribes. People of Torah. People who fear Hashem and tremble before His word. These proper scribes should be appointed in each city and district just like shochtim and butchers are appointed. Anyone who writes a torah scroll, tefillin and mezuzah which is good and proper, as much as he is able, his reward is double and then squared. And he will be saved from the judgments of hell.
2) A sefer torah, tefillin or mezuzah which was written by an apostate should be burnt. Holy writings written by a non-Jew, a מוסר (person who reports on fellow Jews to the government), a women, a deaf person, a mentally handicapped person or a child are invalid and must be stored in a genizah. It is written וקשרתם וכתבתם and it is deduced that all who are obligated בקשירה to tie are also able בכתיבה to write. Anyone not obligated in the tying in not fit for the writing. Since this is deduced from a verse, we require that the person who writes the holy writings be a גדול ממש an adult male who has produced two pubic hairs after reaching the age of 13. If there is any uncertainty, the person is unfit to write until either he has matured or he was found to have a developmental issue when he became twenty years old.
3) Any who are unfit to compose the holy writings are also unfit to correct them. The scribes must be admonished, and punished so that they do not make any corrections to the holy works via women or children.
4) Some say that a sefer torah written by a ממזר is unfit.
5) A sefer torah which was found to be owned by an apostate and it is not known who wrote it, should be put in genizah. If the sefer torah was found to be owned by a non-Jew some say it is kosher and others say it too should be placed in genizah. However, if it was established that the non-Jews plundered sefer torahs from Jews, it is assumed that these too were taken from Jews and are kosher. The same would apply to places where the non-Jews do not known how to write

the holy writings. It is assumed that they plundered them from the Jews. If tefillin were found in the ownership of a non-Jew they are kosher.

6) We do not purchase sefer torah, tefillin or mezuzahs from non-Jews for more than their value. This is to prevent more holy writings from being stolen. However, if the holy writings are offered for sale for their fair market value, one is obligated to purchase the holy writings. If the non-Jew is selling the holy writings for an exorbitant amount, one should try to amicably negotiate the price down to the fair market value. However, if the non-Jew refuses to lower the price, then the holy writings are left in his hands. It is not proper to ask that the non-Jew sell the holy writings at a great discount, because then non-Jew might destroy them.[1]

[1] If he assumes that they are of little value.

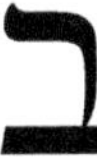

The skin on which they are written
12 sections

1) It is written למען תהיה תורת ה' בפיך "so that the words of Hashem will be in your mouth" and we deduce from here that sefer torah, tefillin and mezuzah can only be written on the skin of domestic animals, wild animals and birds which are pure. Those that are permitted to be placed in your mouth. It is permissible to use, for the holy wriitngs, animals which were neveilah or treifah. It is not required that the actual skin be kosher, but rather that the skin be derived from a specie which could theoretically be kosher. To the exclusion of non-kosher animals. The זוהמא of the fish skin disqualifies it for the holy writings. The skin of a fetus is considered to be a skin and a sefer torah, tefillin and mezuzah may be written on it. This is the best. After comes the skin of the bird and then the skin of the wild animal and then the skin of the domestic animal and then the skin of a neveilah.
2) The skins must be processed לשמה which means that they when they are put into the lime which is the beginning of the process, he must say עורות אלו אני מעבד לשם ספר תורה ולשם זה אני אשים לתוך הסיד "these skins I am processing for the sake of a sefer torah and for this purpose I will place them in the lime." Then they should be placed immediately into the lime. Once the beginning of the processing is לשמה it is assumed that the other work is also לשמה. However, it is proper that at each stage of the production a similar utterance should be said, indicating that the processing is being done לשמה. The same applies to when the skins are first placed into the water so that they will become soft and proper for pressing. The person should say he is place it in the water לשמה. However, בדיעבד, as long as the beginning of the processing was לשמה the skins will be accepted. However, if the beginning of the processing was not done לשמה even though the conclusion of the processing was done לשמה, the skins would not be fit for the holy writings.
3) י"א some say that the words must be uttered verbally, and this is proper לכתחלה. The holiness is not imbued via thoughts but rather as the result of enunciation. Words have a great impact. בדיעבד, one can rely on the authorities who maintain that thoughts are sufficient.
4) Sefer torah, tefillin and mezuzahs are divided in their holiness. The holiness of the sefer torah is greater than the holiness of the tefillin and the holiness of the tefillin is greater than that of the mezuzah. If one intends לשמה for a lighter level of holiness, it would not include a higher level of holiness. קלף which was processed for tefillin would not be kosher for the writing of a sefer torah. However, if one wanted to use this same קלף for holy writings less than tefillin, such as mezuzah, then the לשמה for the higher level of holiness was sufficient. The לשמה of a higher level of holiness, is sufficient for a lighter level of holiness. Some maintain that the skin must be

processed for the specific holy writing for which it is attended. There are also those who question if something dedicated to a higher level of holiness can be used for a lighter level of holiness. Even if one makes a condition there are those who are not sure of the status. Therefore, it is best to process the skins for their specific holy task. That which will be for a sefer torah should be dedicated to a sefer torah. Those that are to be tefillin should be dedicated to tefillin and those that are to be mezuzahs should be dedicated to be tefillin. If this level of dedication is not possible, then one can rely on those who say it is sufficient if at the beginning of the process one says that they are processing the skins for the holiness of a sefer torah and for tefillin, and for mezuzahs and for coverings. Alternatively one can make a conditional statement: עורות אלו אני מעבד לשם קדושת ספר תורה ואני מתנה שאם ארצה לשנות לתפילין או למזוזה או לבתים יהיה הרשות בידי "these skins which I am processing I am doing so for the sake of the holiness of the sefer torah and I condition that if I want to change them to tefillin or mezuzahs or coverings I should have this ability."

5) It is proper to be meticulous in the holiness of the processing in every place where it can be done by a Jew instead of a non-Jew. Even if the Jew does not process them as well as the non-Jew one should consider the view of the Rambam, and those who follow his view, that the skins are invalid if they were processed by a non-Jew. Even if a Jew is supervising and tells him to make the skins לשמה. It is assumed that the non-Jew will have the intentions which he wants to have. However, if there are no Jews able to process the skins, one can rely on the authorities who state that the skins would be kosher if a Jew supervises the non-Jew and tells him to process these skins for a sefer torah etc. It can be assumed that the non-Jew did as the Jew intended. This is only if he commands the non-Jew verbally, and the non-Jew hears. The non verbalized intentions of the Jew are of no consequence for the non-Jew. The Jew must also be present at the moment that the skins are put into the lime and previous instructions are also of no consequence. If the non-Jew has workers which are also non-Jews, these non-Jewish workers must be there when the Jews tells the non-Jew to process the skins לשמה. It is best, if at all possible, the Jew should help the non-Jew at the beginning of the processing, when the skin is first placed into the lime, and the Jew should enunciate that the processing is being done לשמה. This is the tradition. And it would be better if the Jews could assist in all the steps of the processing. בדיעבד even if the Jew did not physically assist at all, the skins would be כשר if the Jew instructed the non-Jew to process the skin לשמה (if the beginning of the processing was not לשמה then even if the Jew did the subsequent processing לשמה the skins would not be permitted).

6) When the skins are processed by the non-Jews the skins should be marked via holes made with needles, in a form similar to the letters. Then we are not concerned that the skins were swapped and the signs were forged, because the non-Jew will be afraid that the Jew will recognize the signs were different than the ones he made or that the Jew will recognize that the signs were made recently. There are those (ברוך שאמר) who say that the signs should not be made with a needle but rather they should be scratched on the top inside of the skin. Also one must be careful because sometimes the non-Jews place their cloth on the holes in skins, and the cloths seal the with other skins not processed לשמה. These patches are difficult to distinguish unless held up to direct sunlight.

7) The skins must be made בעפצא or lime or similar material which causes the skin to contract and thus be strengthened. One must be careful to place the skin in lime until the hairs fall out on their own, and not by scraping. If the skins are pulled early, they are not fit for holy writings but rather are classified as דיפתרא.

8) There are three skins גויל, קלף, and דוכסוסטות. A complete skin after it was processed is called גויל. In ancient times, the tradition was that after the hair was removed from the skin, before the processing, they would divide the skin by its width and it would become two skins. One skin was thin, and it was opposite the hairs and it was called קלף. One was thick and it was opposite the meat and it was called דוכסוסטות. The oral tradition transmitted to Moshe at Sinai was that when the torah scroll was written it was written on the גויל in the place of the hairs and tefillin were written on the קלף in the place of the meat, and the mezuzah was written on the דוכסוסטות in the place of the hairs. Even though this is the oral tradition transmitted to Moshe at Sinai, if one wrote a sefer torah on קלף it is כשר. The גויל was only to exclude דוכסוסטות. Similarly, if one wrote a mezuzah on קלף or on גויל it is כשר. The דוכסוסטות were only said for a mitzvah.

9) Our parchment which is not divided, they have the classification of קלף and we write on the side which previously had the meat. That which we remove the outer layer on the side of the hair is only what is needed to improve and smoothen the parchment. Even if the parchment was divided into two pieces they would have to smooth and scrape it down until only the קלף remained. This parchment is better than גויל and we write on it לכתחילה the sefer torah. In our time we do not write on the גויל and this is permissible also for mezuzah. However, people must be careful to scrape away from the side of the meat so that there will be no small קליפה on the side on which one writes. If there was a קליפה it would be considered דוכסוסטות, and if one wrote on it even one letter, regardless of wheterh it was written for a sefer torah, tefillin or mezuzah the writings are invalid. The way to identify the problematic קליפה is anything which can be separated from the parchment with a needle, even a קליפה as thin as a hair, it would be considered דוכסוסטות.

10) If one veered from what was appropriate and wrote on this parchment on the side which was opposite the hairs, the tefillin, sefer torah or mezuzah would be invalid.

11) If part of the sefer torah was written on גויל and part was written on קלף the sefer torah is invalid because it is considered like two separate scrolls. However, if one made half the scroll גויל and half צבאים , which is the skin of a צבי or other wild animal, even though this is not the best way to accomplish the mitzvah, i.e. it is not מצוה מן המובחר, the writing are kosher.

12) The tradition of some scribes that after processing the parchment in the lime they put a white coloring, called לאג, on the parchment and through this the parchment becomes smooth a brigh white, some say the writings are kosher and some say they are not valid because there is a separation between the writings and the parchment. It is proper to be stringent.

The laws of the ink, the scratches and the quill, and that the writings should be done with the right hand
7 sections

1) The oral tradition given to Moshe at Sinai was that the sefer torah, tefilin and mezuzah can only be written with דיו. The proper way לכתחילה to make the דיו is:

מקבצים עשן של שמנים	
או של זפת	
או של שעוה	
וכיוצא בהם	
וגובלין אותו בשרף אילן	
ובמעט דבש	
ולותחין אותו הרבה	
ודכין אותו עד שיעשה רקיקין	
ומיבשין אותם	
וקודם הכתיבה שורהו במי עפצים וכיוצא בו	
וכותב בו	
שאם תמחקנו יהיה נמחק	

This is the דיו which is ideal מצוה מן המובחר for the writing of sefer torah, tefillin and mezuzah. If they were all written במי עפצים and קנקנתום which is permanent and is not erased they are kosher. This is the tradition now to make the דיו even לכתחילה with מי עפצים, קומום and קנקנתום. However one must be careful that they are black. IF they are not black what was excluded by the oral tradition given to Moshe at Sinai that the holy writings must be written with דיו. It was to exclude other colors such as red and green etc. If one wrote even one letter with some other color or gold, the writings are not valid. Therefore, it is forbidden to write any names of the תנ"ך with anything other than דיו. Some say that דיו is only required for a sefer torah.

2) Even if the writings were originally written with black דיו and after time the דיו deteriorated and became red, the writings are invalid. This is a common occurance and one must be careful.
3) The דיו does not need to be made לשמה and if it was made from סתם יינם (regular non-kosher wine) there is no prohibition. However, for matters of holiness and for the writing of the divine name it is proper to sanctify ourselves with that which is permitted to us and to avoid that which is inappropriate[2] and that which is similar to that which is inappropriate.

[2] The term used by the Keset Sofer is נכון לקדש עצמינו במותר לנו ולהרחיק מן הכיעור ומן הדומה לו

4) If one sprinkled gold dust on the letters, if the gold is removed and the letters underneath remain, it is kosher. This would apply even to tefillin and mezuzah.[3] However, if one threw gold on אות מאזכרה (the divine name etc.) there is no way the holy writings can be corrected since it is forbidden to remove the gold. Removing the gold would be the prohibition of erasing the divine name.
5) The tradition given to Moshe at Sinai was that sefer torah, tefillin and mezuzah must have scratched lines, and if there were no scratched lines they are invalid. And it must be scratched with something that is sharp and makes scratches. It should not be scratched with lead, since this colors it. One must be careful to make the scratches לשמה. If there was error in the writings, and the letters was scraped away and the scratches were erased, that place must be scratched anew. Similarly, if a word or words in the sefer torah is left handing between the lines, scratches must be made there. Regarding the tefillin, only the top line must be scratched. There are those who say that the top and bottom of the line must be scratched and from both sides. This applies even if one is able to write without the scratches. If one does not know how to write straight lines without scratches, each line must be scratched.
6) The קולמוס even though after it finished its job it is not recognized in the writings, a קולמוס נאה beautiful קולמוס should be used. There are those who say one should write with a קולמוס made from a reed and not a feather, but this is not the tradition. We use a קולמוס made from a feather and even one made from iron. There is a question[4] whether one can used a קולמוס made from the feather of a non-pure bird.
7) The writings must be done with the right hand, and if they were done with the left hand they are invalid. If the only pair of tefillin are those written with the left hand, and the person is unable to find other tefillin written with the right hand, he may wear the left hand written tefillin without a blessing. A person who is left handed, his left hand is his right hand. If a left handed person wrote with his right hand, the writings are invalid. If a person is ambidextrous the person should write with his right hand, and if he wrote with his left hand the writings are kosher. If a person writes with his left hand, and everything else is done with the right hand, he should not be accepted as a scribe. בדיעבד if he wrote, the writings are kosher just as is the case by one who is ambidextrous. There was an incident with a person who was גדם and he grabbed the קולמוס with his lip and wrote, and his writings were deemed invalid. The writings were deemed invalid even if there was no alternative since the normal way of writing is not with the mouth.

[3] Which must be written in order.
[4] Which is apparently unresolved.

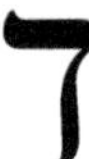

That the writing must be done לשמה and other laws of writings and not to turn over the sheet
11 sections

1) A sefer torah, tefillin and mezuzah must be written with great concentration. They must be written לשמה and one must enunciate his intentions prior to the writings. For example before beginning to write a sefer torah the person must say: "ספר זה אני כותב לשם קדושת ספר תורה this scroll I am writing for the sanctity of seger torah." This declaration is sufficient for the entire scroll (with the exception of the holy names which the scribe must specifically sanctify). Similarly, for tefillin or mezuzah one should say: לשם קדושת תפילין or לשם קדושת מזוזה. If one did not enunciate this declaration with their mouth, rather they had this intention in their heart some invalidate the writings even בדיעבד. Some permit these writings בדיעבד and they seem to be the more accepted view.
2) When one is dozing they should not write because at that time he is not writing with the proper concentration. Similarly, if one consumes alcoholic beverages, one should not write because they will not have the proper concentration.
3) Every single letter must be written לשמה, even if just a small part of the writings was not written לשמה but the majority was written the לשמה the writings are invalid. All the more so, if some part was not accomplished through writing but rather by a drop of דיו falling, and this drop became a letter, that these writings are not valid. Even if after this the קולמוס is passed over each letter לשמה this does not rectify the situation, the additional writings do not help.[5]
4) Before one begins writing it is proper to test the קולמוס, that there should not be extra ink which could ruin the writings.
5) When writing a sefer torah, there must be another scroll in front of the scribe. This other scrolls should be a proper scroll from which the scribe can copy. It is forbidden to write even one letter שלא מן הכתב. Therefore, each scribe should be certain that he has a corrected scroll,[6] which was validated, that he can copy from. However, the scribe does not need to view each word on its own, rather he should do in the manner of those who copy. Two or three words should be copied at the same time, depending on the comfort level of the scribe. It is forbidden to write even one letter of a sefer torah שלא מן הכתב. If even one letter was written שלא מן כתב some say it is forbidden to read from the scroll שלא בשעת הדחק unless there is great urgency. Some say בדיעבד the writings are not invalid.

[5] Even though the quill with ink was passed over letters that had been written through some invalid member, and there is now theoretically proper writing covering the improper writings, the writings are not valid.
[6] The Keset Sofer calls this a חומש.

6) Even though the sefer torah is written מתוך הכתב each word must be enunciated before it is written, so that there will not be any mistakes and also so that the sanctity of the reading of each word coming from the scribes mouth should be on the letters. However, manners of rebuke דברי פורעניות do not need to be enunciated.
7) One should be careful with extra and missing letters.[7] If one wrote an extra or lacking letter, the writings are invalid. A word which is קרי וכתיב like that which is written ישגלנה and is read ישכבנה, it is written ובעפולים and read ובטחורים and similar instances must be written as they are written, and if one changed and wrote the words the way they are read the writings are invalid.
8) Regarding the writing of tefillin and mezuzahs: if the chapters roll off his tongue,[8] they may be written שלא מן הכתב (by heart). However, each word must be enunciated.
9) A scribe is only allowed to write מתוך הכתב if he knows to read. If the scribe does not know to read, even though he knows how to write all the letters, he can easily make a mistake and not be aware of his error.
10) One can take דיו from the letter which was already written, to write another letter. He may even discard the extra דיו if the scribe needs the letters to dry faster so he can roll the scroll. However, this דיו which was used to write a holy letter can not be used for mundane writing. If the extra דיו is in the divine name, then the דיו may not be taken even if he wants to use the דיו to write a different divine name. However, if more than a normal amount of דיו was used, there is room to be lenient, even to discard the extra דיו. Originally, the only sanctity applied to the דיו was what was necessary for the writings. The additional דיו is detrimental to the writings.
11) Scribes of sefer torahs, tefillin and mezuzahs who want to leave the sheet so that it will dry, should not leave the sheet face down, even though the scribe's intention tis that the dust will not go on the holy writings. Leaving the sheet with the holy writings face down, is disrespectful to the holy writings. The writings should be face up and a cloth should be spread over it, or it should be doubled over. However, if there is no other option it can be left face down because if there is no option there will be a greater disrespect to the writings.

---

[7] Primarily the letter vuv.
[8] That is the scribe is very familiar with the chapters and knows the chapters by heart.

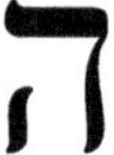

The shape of the letters and the zayins
6 sections

1) לכתחילה one must write with a nice and straight script. The penmanship should clearly depict the entire shape of each letter, for the shapes of the letters were deduced from Talmudic and Midrashic sources, and traditions from the Reishonim Z"L. However, if the shape was slightly changed, the writings are not invalid is long as the letters retain their shape.
2) These are the shapes of the letters:

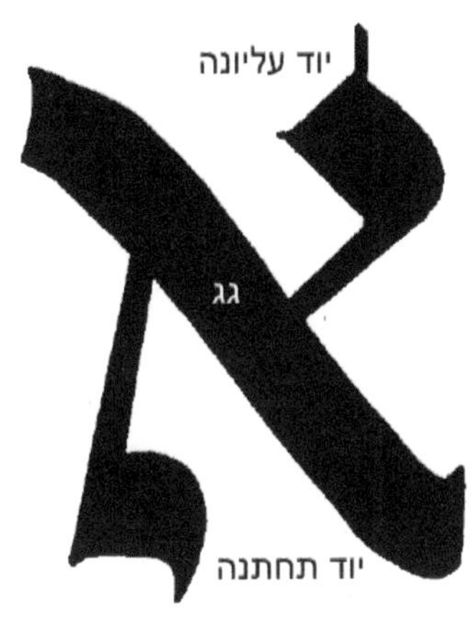

א צריכה להיות הנקודה העליונה	The alef must have its upper part	
עשויה כעין יו"ד	Shaped to resemble a yud	
וצריך להיות בה עוקץ אחד למעלה לכתחלה	And there must be an עוקץ above לכתחלה	
ואחד למטה	And one below	
מימין	On the right	
הנוגע בגג האלוף	Which touches the גג of the alef	
ואם לאו פסולה כמשי"ת	And if not it is invalid as will be explained	

ויו"ד זו צריך להיות לכתחלה שתהא פניה עם העוקץ שלמעלה הפוך קצת כלפי מעלה	This yud must be לכתחלה, together with the עוקץ facing slightly upwards	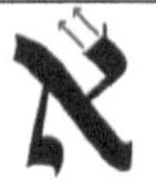
וקבלה מהחסיד שתהא רגל יו"ד זו	There is a tradition from the righteous that the foot of this yud	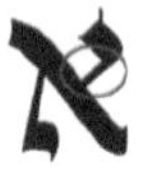
נוגעת לכתחלה באמצע גג	Should attached to the middle of the גג	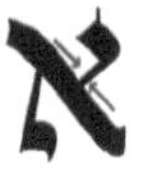
ולא בקצהו	And not at its end	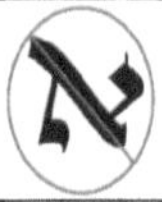
וסוף הגג של צד ימין	And the end of the גג on the right side	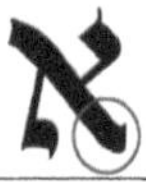
צריך לכתחלה שיהא עקום קצת כלפי מעלה	Must be slightly slanted upwards	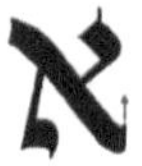
ולא יהא עקום הרבה	But it should not be slanted too much	
ונקודה התחתונה פעמים שתמונתה כדל"ת קטנה הפוכה עפ"י הסוד וכן צריך להיות בתפילין עפ"י קבלת האר"י ז"ל	Sometimes the image of the bottom part is like a small daled, inverted according to the סוד. This is the way it must be in tefillin according to the Ari Z"L	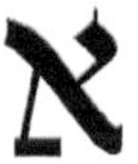
ופעמים שתמונתה גם כן כיו"ד תלויה בגגה	Sometimes it resembles a yud hung by its גג	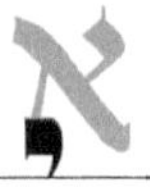
ולכן לכתחלה צריך שיהא לה עוקץ קטן לצד ימין למטה	לכתחלה it must have a small עוקץ on the right side at the bottom	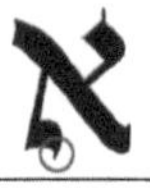
ועפ"י הסוד צריך שיהא עוקץ זה מכוון כנגד העוקץ העליון שעל היו"ד העליונה	According to the סוד this עוקץ must be opposite the top עוקץ which is on the upper yud	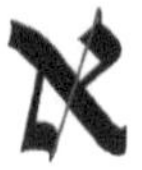
(אם יודי האלוף נוגעין בגגה דהיינו בקו האמצעי יותר מן הראוי ע"ל סי ח)	(if the yuds of the alef are attached to the גג, which is the middle line, more than appropriate see chapter 8)	
אם כתב יו"ד העליונה הפוכה כזה	If one wrote the upper yud backwards like this	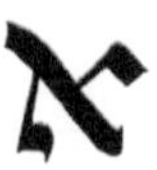
אם אפשר לתקן בנקל יתקן	If it can be easily corrected, it should be corrected	

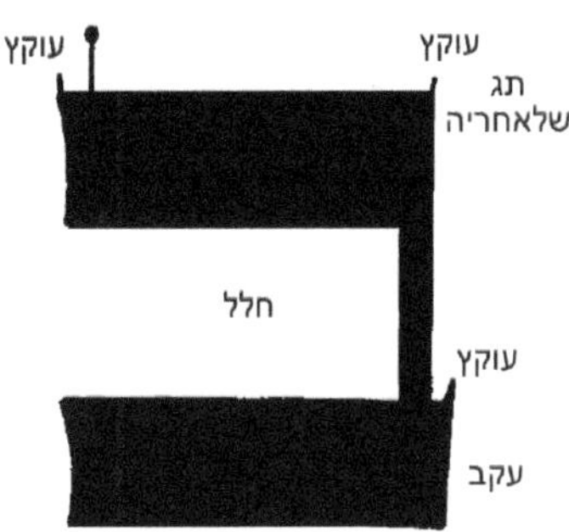

ב' צריך ליזהר בתג שלאחריה לרבעה	The beis should have a תג in the back to make it square	
שלא תהא נראית ככא"ף	So that it does not resemble a kof	
ואם נראית ככא"ף פסולה	And if it appears like a kof it is invalid	
ואם ספק מראין לתינוק	If one is uncertain they show it to a youngster[1]	
ולכתחלה צריך שיהא לה בגגה מצד ימין עוקץ קטן	לכתחלה there must be an עוקץ קטן on the right side of the גג	
נוטה לצד ימין	Bending towards the right	
ועוקץ קטן מצד שמאל	And an עוקץ קטן on the left	
זקוף למעלה	facing upwards	
ועפ"י הקבלה יהא לה עקב עב למטה	According to the kabala, it should have a thick עקב on the bottom	

[1] The letter is shown to a youngster who is neighter smart nor foolish, and at the age where they are just learning to read. Thus they can identify the letters, but would not be able to derive contextual clues. The child is then asked to identify the letter.

כי תמונתה כמו דל"ת תוך גרון של וא"ו	Its image is that like a daled in the throat of a vuv	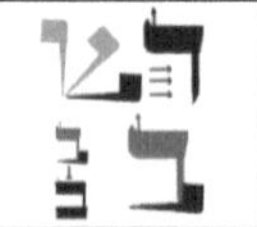
ע"כ צריך שיהא לה זוית למעלה	Therefore it must have corners above,	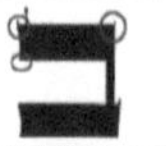
שתהא כמו דל"ת	So that it resembles the daled	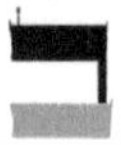
ועקב טוב למטה שיהא במקום ראשה של וא"ו	And a proper עקב below in the place of the head of the vuv	
ויהיה ארכה ורחבה כג' קולמסים ורוחב חללה כעובי קולמס	The length and width should be three quill lengths and the empty open space should be the width of a quill.	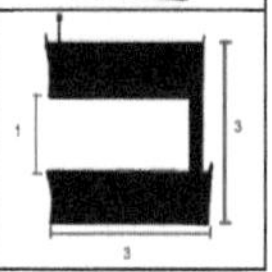

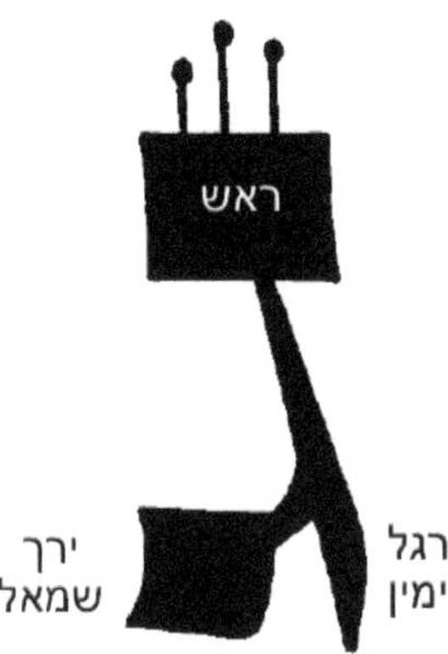

ג' צריך שיהא ראשה עב	The gimel should have a thick head	
ורגל ימין יהא דק לכתחלה	And לכתחלה the right foot should be thin	
ויורד למטה מעט יותר מירך שמאל	It[2] should go down lower than the left foot	
וירך שמאל לא תהיה עקומה	And the left foot should not be crooked	
אלא משיכה בשוה	Rather drawn straight	
ומוגבהת קצת כלפי דל"ת לכתחלה	לכתחלה it should be raised slightly towards the daled[3]	
וקבלה בידי רבותינו הראשונים ז"ל שגוף הגימ"ל יהיה כמו זיי"ן	There was a tradition among our masters the Reishonim that the body of the gimel should be like a zayin	
שימשוך רגל ימין מאמצע הראש	that the right foot should be drawn from the middle of the head	

[2] The thin right foot should go down lower than the left foot.

[3] The לשכת סופר notes that the idea here is based on the Talmud that the גומלי חסדים, those who do good deeds run after the דלים the poor. למעשה the bottom of the gimel should be raised slightly towards where the daled would be if the alfa bet was written out.

ולא מקצהו כמו בוא"ו	And not from the end like the vuv	
וכן כל ראש שמאל שבאותיות שעטנ"ז ג"ץ יהיו דומין לזיין	And the same is with all left heads among the letters שטנ"ז ג"ץ should resemble the zayin ש ע ט נ ז ג ץ ן צ	
וע"כ התגין שעליהן נקראו זיונין	Therefore, the תג on top of them are called זיונין zayinun.	
אבל קבלת האר"י ז"ל אינו כן כמשי"ת	However, this is not the tradition of the Ari Z"L.	
וירך שמאל תהא נמוכה	The left ירך should be deeper	
כדי להסמיך אות אצל ראשה	So that other letters can be next to its head[4]	
כי כן קבלה מהחסיד שכשיכתוב וא"ו אצל נו"ן כפופה יכתבנה בתוך כפיפת הנו"ן כדי להסמיך ראשיהן זה אצל זה	This is the tradition of the Rightious One that when the vuv is written adjacent to the nun kefufa it should be written inside the doubling over of the nun so that the heads will be adjacent to each other[5]	
וכשיכתוב כא"ף פשוטה אצל צדי"ק כפופה טוב לעקם צואר הצדיק מעט לצד ימין	And when the kaf peshuta is written next to a tzadik kefufa it is best to slightly bend the neck of the tzadik to the right	
כדי שיקרב קצת כא"ף הפשוטה לראש הצדיק	So that the the kaf peshuta will be closer to the head of the tzadik	
אבל בלי צורך לא יעקם שום אות כי כן קבלה מהראשונים שיהיו כולם בעמידה פשוטים ולא מוטים לא לימין ולא לשמאל	However, without need no letter should be bent for this is the tradition from the Reishonim, that all the letters should be straight and not slanted neither to the right nor to the left.	

[4] So that other letters can be next to head of the gimel.

[5] The Lishkat Sofer includes a descriptive image which are reproduced here. The top image בנו where the vuv is adjacent to the nun is considered not proper, while the bottom בנו image is considered proper.

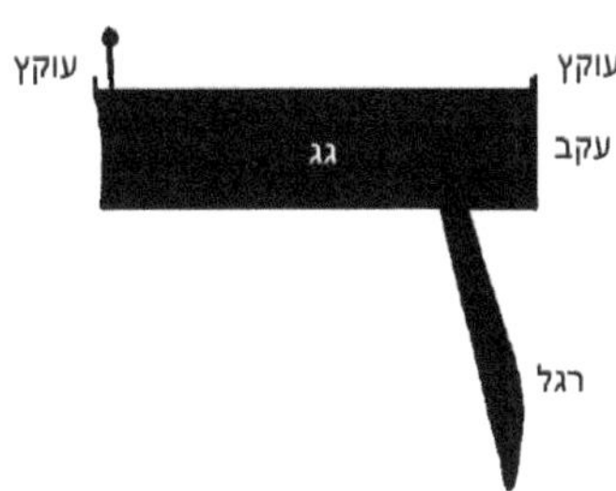

ד' צריך שיהא גגה ארוך	The daled should have a long גג	
ורגלה קצר	And a short רגל	
שאם יהיה רגלה ארוך מגגה תדמה לכא"ף פשוטה ותפסל כשלא יקראנה התינוק כראוי	If the רגל is longer than the גג the daled will resemble a kaf peshuta and will be invalid when the child will not identify it properly	
וצריך שיהיה הרגל פשוט	And the רגל must be straight	
בשיפוע קצת לצד ימין	Slightly slanted to the right	
ושיהא לה תג קטן בראש גגה מצד שמאל	And it should have a small תג on the left top of the גג	
וצריך ליזהר בתג שלאחוריה	And one must be careful with the תג in the back	
לרבעה	To make it square[6]	
שלא תהא נראית כמו רי"ש ותפסול על ידי קריאת התינוק	So that it will not resemble a reish and be invalid if the child will not identify it properly	
ויש מי שקבלה בידו שלכתחלה אינו די במה שיהא לה זוית חד מלאחוריה	And there are those who have a tradition that לכתחלה it is not sufficient that the daled have sharp corners in the back[7]	
אלא יהא לה שם עקב טוב לכתחלה	Rather לכתחלה it should have a proper עקב	
כי תמונתה כמו ב' ווי"ן סגורים	For its image is like two closed vuvs	

[6] The difference between the reish and the daled is the square part of the back of the daled. Although, many sofrim have the tradition to extend the back (עקב) of the daled so that it will be impossible to confuse with a reish, the daled lacking the distinct back extension can very easily be confused with the reish. Two examples of such daleds are presented at the right.

[7] As already discussed in the previous footnote, the daled does not need the exaggerated end, used in the daleds depicted here. Really, it is sufficient for the letter to be square in the back.

והעקב הוא נגד ראש וא"א אחד	And the עקב is in place of the heads of one of the vuvs	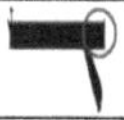
ויעשה גם כן עוקץ קטן לצד ימין בולט על פניה למעלה	And a small עוקץ should also be made on the right side facing upwards	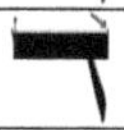
ועוקץ זה הוא כנגד ראש הוא"ו השני:	And this עוקץ corresponds with the head of the second vuv	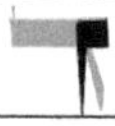

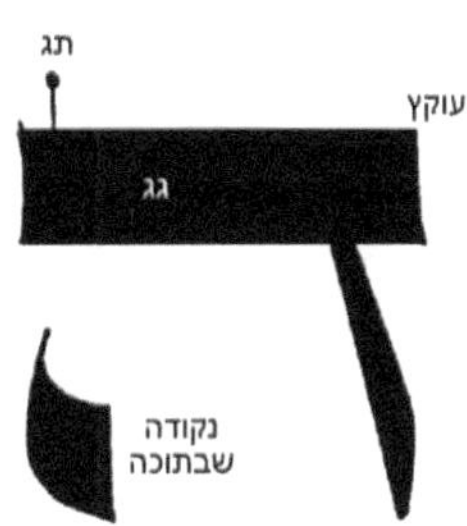

ה' צריך לעשות לה לכתחלה תג קטן למעלה לצד שמאל	לכתחלה the heh should have a small תג on the upper left	
וגם באחוריה יעשה עוקץ קטן	Also in the back there should be a small עוקץ	
שתהא מרובעת כדל"ת	So that it will be square like a daled	
ולא עגולה כרי"ש	And not round like a reish	
והנקודה שבתוכה לא תהיה סמוכה לגגה	And the נקודה שבתוכה the dot in the middle should not be close to the גג	
אלא יהא ביניהם חלק כל כך בכדי שאדם בינוני יכירנו היטב מעל ספר תורה שעל גבי הבימה כשקורא בה	Rather it should be sufficiently spaced so that a normal person will recognize it when reading from a sefer torah which is on the podium, as it is being read	
ואם נגעה ממש בגגה אפילו נגיעה דקה כחוט השערה פסולה	If the dot is actually touching the גג even a slight touch, the writings are invalid	
ולא תהא הנקודה נגד אמצע הגג	The dot should not be in the middle of the גג	
אלא נגד סופו בצד שמאל	Rather it should be towards the ends on the left side	
ואם עשאה באמצע פסולה	If it was made in the middle it is invalid	
וצריך לתקנה אלא אם כן אין תיקון מועיל אזי יש להכשיר אפילו לכתחלה	And it must be corrected. If a correction will not possible then it is kosher לכתחלה.	
(ע' מג"עא ס' ל"ב ס"ק ל"ג ונ"ל דייכ"פ יש להבחין על ידי תינוק אם קוראת כראוי)	(see the MA 32:33 that one must see if it is correctly identified by a child)	
ויש מי שקבלה בידו שהנקודה תהא דקה מלמעלה	There are those who have a tradition that the dot should be thin towards the top	
ועבה קצת מלמטה כעין יו"ד הפוכה	And wide, lower down, like an inverted yud	
כי תמונת הה"א היא דל"ת ויו"ד	The image of the heh is a daled and yud	
(בכל ההי"ן חוץ מההי"ן של שם	(in all the hehs except the hehs of the blessed divine	

הוי"ה ברוך הוא שיש בהן קבלה אחרת)	name, which has a different tradition)	
ותהא הנקודה עקומה למטה לצד ימין	And the dot should be slanted downward towards the right	
ולא לצד שמאל פן תדמה לתי"ו	And it should not be slanted towards the left so it does not resemble a tav.	

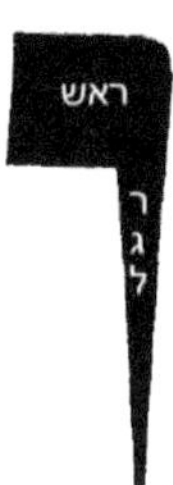

ו' צריך לעשות ראשה קצר	The head of the vuv must be short	
שלא תדמה לרי"ש	So that it does not resemble a reish	
ורגלה ארוך	And the foot should be long	
שלא תדמה ליו"ד על ידי קריאת התינוק	So that it does not resemble a yud, when read by the child	
וטוב שתהיה עגולה לצד ימין בראשה	It is best that it should be round on the right side of the head	
שלא תדמה לזיי"ן	So that it does not resemble a zayin	
ואעפ"י שראש הזיי"ן עובר משיני צדדין מכל מקום יש לחוש שמא התינוק יקראנה זיי"ן ותפסול	And even though the head of the zayin goes over on both sides, there is still concern that the child will identify it as a zayin[8] and the writings will be invalid	
ועל פי הסוד צריך לעשות רגלה פשוט בשוה	According to the סוד the foot must be straight	
ועוביו מתעט והולך מעט מעט עד שתהא חדה למטה	And the width diminishes as it goes down until it is sharp on the bottom	
ועל פי קבלת האר"י ז"ל צריך להיות עוקץ קטן מצד שמאל בראש כל הווי"ן שבתפילין ולא כספר תורה	According to the tradition of the Ari ZL there must be a small עוקץ on the left head of the vuvs in tefillin, not in the sefer torah.	

[8] i.e. If the vuv is square, even though the head does not extend over both parts of the foot, it might be confused with a zayin.

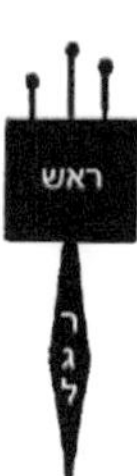

ז' צריך ליזהר שלא יהא רגלה ארוך	The zayin should not have a long leg	
שלא תדמה לנו"ן פשוטה ותפסול על ידי קריאת התינוק	So that it will not resemble a nun peshuta and be invalid as a result of the reading of the child	
וראשה צריך להיות עובר מב' הצדדין	The head must over hang on the two sides[9]	
שלא תדמה לוא"ו	So that it will not resemble a vuv	
ויהיה מרובע על פי הסוד	There is a סוד tradition that the zayin be square.	

[9] That is the head must overhang the two sides of the foot.

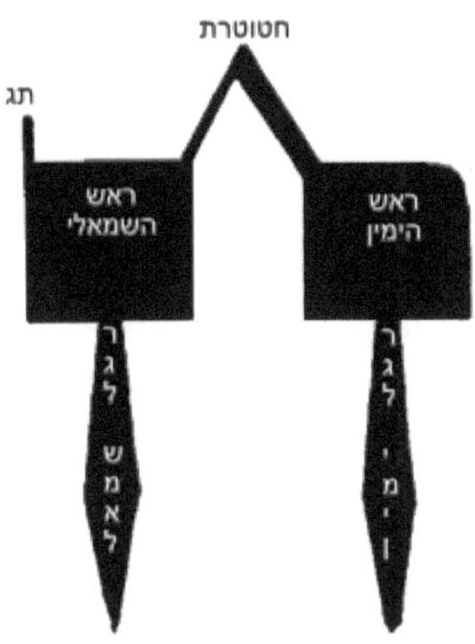

ח' לכתחלה צריך לעשות שתי זייני"ן	לכתחלה the ches should be made of two zayins	
(ביניהן כעובי קולמס)	The space between equal to a קולמס	רחב קלמוס
והזיי"ן הראשונה יהיה ראשה עגול בצד ימין	And the first zayin will have the top right rounded	
וחטוטרת על גביהן המחברן	And a חטוטרת on top to attach them	

וגם תג קטן בראש השמאלי	And also a small תג on the head of the left[10]	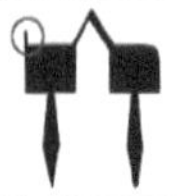
ועל פי קבלת האר"י ז"ל צריך לעשות רגל הימיני כמו וא"ו בתפילין	And according to the tradition of the Ari Z"L the foot of the right must be like a vuv in tefillin	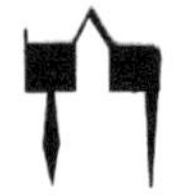
וקו החטוטרת שעל רגל הימין	And the line of the חטוטרת on the right foot	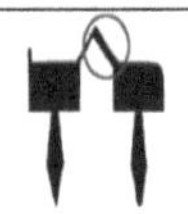
יהיה עב	Should be thick	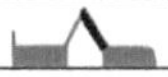
ושעל רגל השמאלי יהיה דק	And on the left foot[11] should be thin	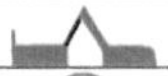
ולא יאריך בגגה כלל	And the גג should not be elongated at all	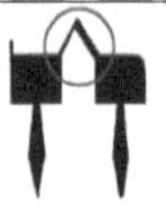
ואם האריך דהיינו שעשה ב' זייני"ן רחוקין	And if he elongated, that is he made two zayins a distance apart	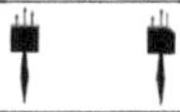
וגג רחב פסולה משום דלא הוי חטוטרת	And a wide גג, the writings are <u>invalid</u>[12] because it is not a חטוטרת	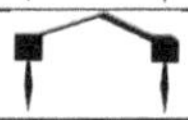
ובתפילין ומזוזה אין לה תיקון	In tefillin and mezuzah there is no way to correct this	
אבל אם עשאה כדעת רש"י בלא חטוטרת	However, if he wrote according to the view of Rashi, without the [13]חטוטרת	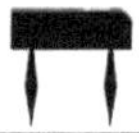
(כמו שהיא בכתב ספרדית הנקרא וועליש)	(the ways it is in the ספרדי writings known as וועליש)	
אפילו האריך בה כשרה בדיעבד	Even if he made it longer it is kosher בדיעבד	
אף על פי שאינה מרובעת	Even though it is not square	
וכן אם עשאה ד' וזיי"ן	Similarly, if he made a daled and a zayin	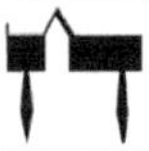
וחטוטרת על גבה פסולה	And the חטוטרת is on top, the writings are not valid	

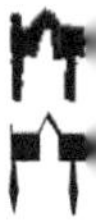

[10] The Lishkat Sofer (gloss 10) notes the various views among the Reishonim for this תג. There was an ancient tradition to put this תג in the middle of the head and almost make it appear as a crown. The Lishkat Sofer quotes the Bies Yosef that the placement of תג must be clear that it is not like a crown.
The Lishkat Sofer also notes what is assumed to be the view of the Bali Tosefos how to make a ches. There ches had a right zayin and a left vuv. The picture of published in the the Lishkat Sofer is to the right (upper) and the fixed up clearer version is below it.
[11] That is the line of the חטוטרת which is on the left foot should be thin.
[12] See the Lishkat Sofer who quotes the Chassam Sofer that there is room to be lenient in this regard.
[13] The Lishkat Sofer notes that if some of the ches have the חטוטרת and others do not, this is not a problem. Even Rashi would agree that the ches with the חטוטרת is kosher.

ומכל מקום אם נמצא כן בספר תורה בשבת או בתמונת ב' ווי"ן	If it was found like this[14] in a sefer torah on shabbas or an image of two vuvs	
וחטוטרת על גביהן אין להוציא אחרת	And there is a חטוטרת on top of them, there is no need to take out another sefer torah	

Additional Writings:

According to the Lishkas Sofer there was a ches which was written with extra base on the bottom (the image from the printed version is to the left and the manipulated one is to the right). This ches is also prominent is Sefer Hatagin. Although it is not apparent from Sefer Hatagin that it was used for all ches, it was in some most noteable in the verse וחרה אף.		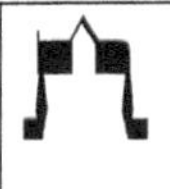

[14] i.e. the ches resembles and image of a daled and zaying instead of two zayins.

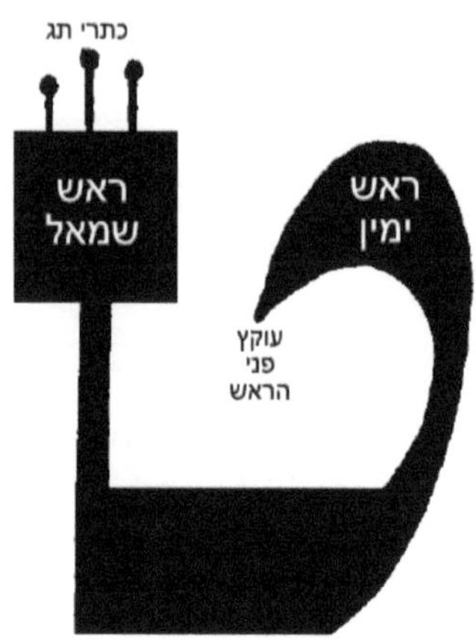

ט' צריך שיהא ראש ימין שלה קצת ארוך ועגול	The right head of the tes must be a bit long and round	
ועוקץ פני הראש הזה כפוף	And the עוקץ of the head should be bent	
מעט למטה לכתחלה	לכתחלה a bit downward	
אבל לא יהא כפוף הרבה לכתחלה	לכתחלה it should not be bent a great deal	
וגם למטה יעשנה עגולה	And also below it should be round	
(כי תמונתה כמו כ"ף וזיי"ן)	(because the image is one of a kaf and a zayin)	
וראש שמאל שלה יהיה כמו זיי"ן	And the left head should be like a zayin	
(לדברי המצריכין כן בכל אותיות שעטנ"ז ג"ץ אבל לפי קבלה האר"י ז"ל תהיה כוא"ו ישרה בתפילין)	(According to those who need this in all the letters of שעטנ"ז ג"ץ. However, according to the tradition of the Ari Z"L it should be like a straight vuv in the tefillin.)	
אבל ראש ימין יהיה לכתחלה עגול כמו שאמרנו	However, the right head should לכתחלה be round as we said	
ולא יהא ראוי להושיב עליב כתרי התגין	And it should not be such that the crowns of the תגין can be placed on it[15]	
שאם ראש הראשון היה שוה וראוי לתגין כמו ראש השני לא היו מדלגין	If the first head was equal and fit for the תגין, like the	

[15] That is the head should be bent so that the there is no flat surface for the crowns to be placed.

עליו להושיבם בראש השני דומה למה שאמרו אין מעבירין על המצות	second head we could not skip it to put them on the second head as we said that one should not pass on the מצות	
ומטעם זה כל היודי"ן שבצד ימין בעי"ן וצדי"ק ושי"ן שבספר תורה כולם פניהם כלפי מעלה ואינם ראויין להושיב עליהן כתרי התגין	For this reason all the yuds which are on the right side of the ayin, tzadik and shin in the sefer torah, all face upwards so that they are not fit to place the crown of the תגין	

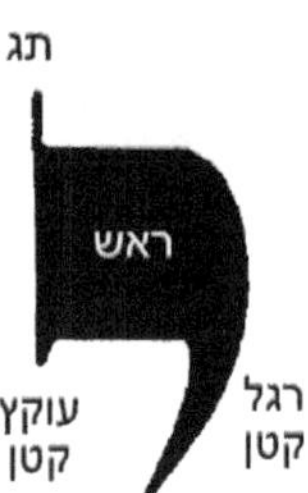

י' צריך להיות לה רגל קטן מימן	The yud must have a small foot on the right	
ותג קטן מלמעלה בצד שמאל לכתחלה	And לכתחלה a small תג above on the left side	
וצריך לעשות ראשה כפוף בשמאלו למטה	And the head must be bent on the lower left[16]	
ויהיה כמו עוקץ קטן יורד למטה	And there should be a small עוקץ pointing downward	
ויהיה עוקץ זה קצר מרגלה שבימינה	And this עוקץ should be shorter then the right foot	
פן תדמה לחי"ת	Otherwise it might resemble a ches	
ויהיה הרגל קטן ולא גדול	And the foot should be small and not large	
פן תדמה לרי"ש	Otherwise it might resemble a reish	
או לוא"ו ותפסל על ידי קריאת התינוק	Or a vuv and the writings will be invalid through the reading of the child	
ונכון שיהיה הרגל כפוף קצת לכתחלה להטיב צורתה	And it is proper that the foot should לכתחלה be a bit bent to improve the form	

[16] While the עוקץ or תג on top rises sharply from the top of the yud, the עוקץ on the bottom should be the result of the curvature of the bottom left of the top of the yud.

אם חסר עוקצה השמאלי ומכ"ש רגלה הימיני פסולה	If the left עוקץ is missing, and all the more so the right foot the writings are invalid.	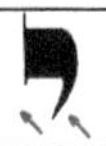

Additional Writings:

According to the Mishnas Sofrim the top right of the yud should be rounded.		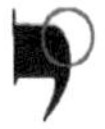
There are those who do not have the lower עוקץ.		
There are those who have a more dramatic תג.		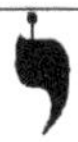

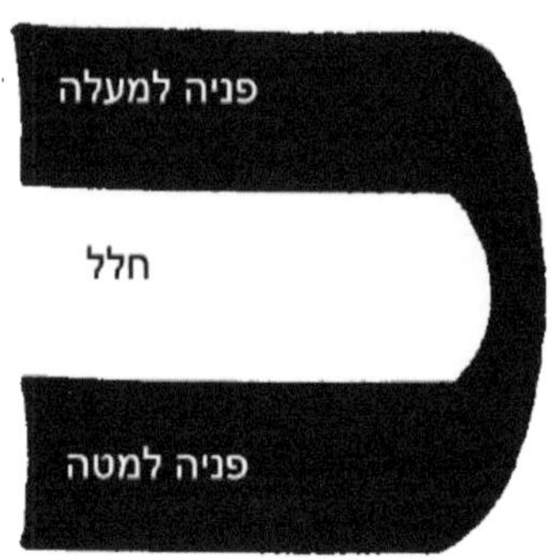

כ' כפופה קבלת החסיד שצריכה להיות עגולה מכל צד ולא יהא לה שום זוית לכתחלה	Regarding the kaf kefufa there is a tradition from the righteous one, that it must be round on all sides and לכתחלה it should not have any corners	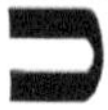
ואם עשה לה זוית באחוריה מלמעלה כשרה	And if corners were made in the upper right (the back) it is kosher	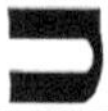
אם היא עגולה מלמטה	As long as it is round on the bottom right	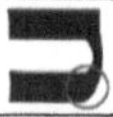
אבל אם עשה לה זוית מלמטה הרי זו דומה לבי"ת ופסולה	However, if there was a corner on the bottom right, it will resemble a beis and the writings will be invalid	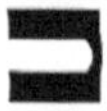
ויש אומרים דכל שיש לה זוית למעלה	And there are those who say that anything which has corners either above	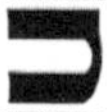
או למטה פסולה	Or below, the writing are invalid	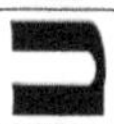
ותהיה פניה למעלה ולמטה שוים	The upper and lower lines should be equal	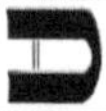
ורוחב חללה כעובי קולמס	And the width of the open space should be the width of a קולמס	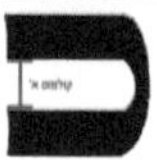

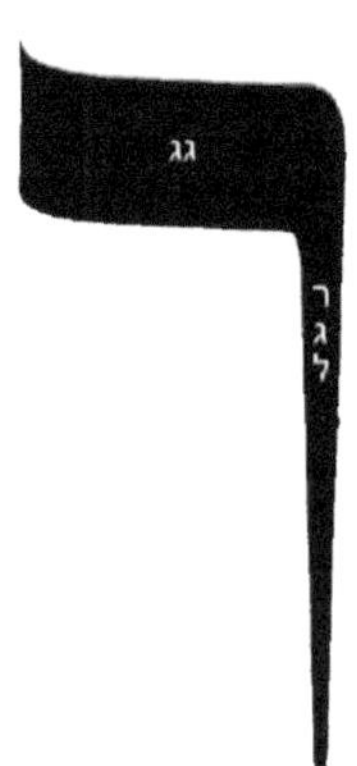

ך' פשוטה צריך לעשות גגה קצר	The kaf peshuta must have a small גג	
שלא תדמה לרי"ש	So that it does not resemble the letter reish	
לכן לא ימשוך אותה בסוף שיטה	Therefore it should not be drawn out at the end of a line	
ואף על פי שכל האותיות אין למושכן מכל מקום בדיעבד כשרות אבל זו פסולה אם התינוק אינו קוראה כהלכתה	And even though all the letters should not be drawn out, בדיעבד they are kosher, but this letter is invalid if the child does not read it appropriately	
ולכתחלה צריך לעשות כל הפשוטות ארוכות כשיעור	לכתחלה all the peshutas should be the proper length	
שאם היו נכפלו היו כפופות	That if they were doubled over, they would be kefufos	

ומטעם זה לא יעשה לכא"ף פשוטה זוית למעלה	For this reason a person should not make upper corners on the kaf peshuta	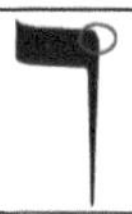
אלא תהא עגולה כמו רי"ש	Rather it should be round like a reish	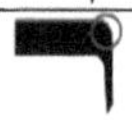
שאם היו כופפין אותה היתה כא"ף כפופה	That if it was doubled over, it would be a kaf kefufa	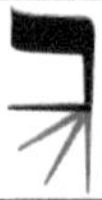
שאין חילוק ביניהם אלא שזו כפופה וזו פשוטה	For there is no difference between them, except one is a kefufa and one is a peshuta	
ואם עשה לה זוית למעלה	If a corner was made above	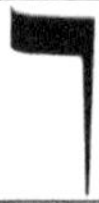
כמו דל"ת	Similar to the daled	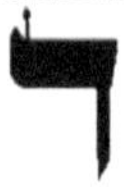
יש פוסלין ויש מכשירין ויש לסמוך עליהם בדיעבד	There are those who invalidated the writings, and those who permit the writings, and the latter can be relied upon בדיעבד	

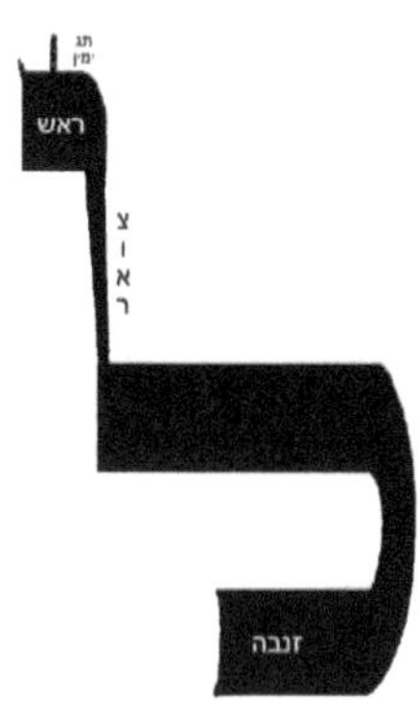

ל' צריך להיות צוארה ארוך	The lamed must have a long neck	
כמו וא"ו	Like a vuv	
וראשה עגול לצד ימין	And the head is round on the right side	
ולצד שמאל זוית לראשה	And on the left side there is a corner to the head	
כמו ראש וא"ו	Like the head of a vuv	
כי תמונת הלמ"ד היא כמו כא"ף כפופה	The image of the lamed is a kof kefufa	

ועליה וא"ו	With a vuv on top	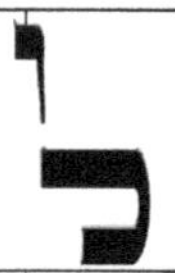
ומטעם זה יהיה זנבה עב	And for this reason the tail should be thick	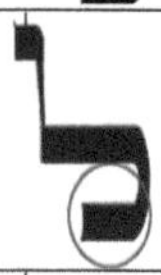
וכפוף היטב לפניה	And bent over well in front	
ותהיה עגולה מאחוריה לצד ימין	And it should be round in the back on the right	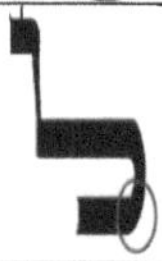
כמן כא"ף כפופה	Like a kof kefufa	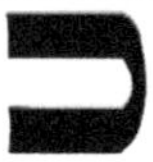
אבל לצד שמאל מקום חיבור הגוף עם הצואר	But on the right side, where the body connects to the neck	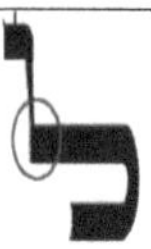
יהיה לה זוית בין סוף הוא"ו שיורד בדקות לצורת כא"ף	It should have a corner between the end of the vuv that narrows toward the kof	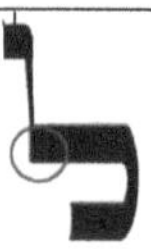
וכל זה לכתחלה ועל פי הסוד צריך לעשות לה שני תגין על ראש צוארה	All of this is לכתחלה, according to the סוד there should be two תגין on the top of the neck	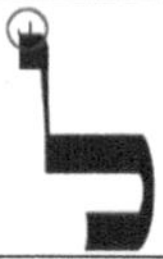
הימיני גבוה מעט	The right תג higher	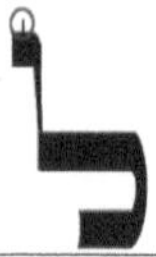
והשמאלי נמוך ממנו	And the left תג lower	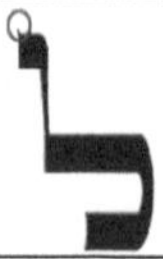

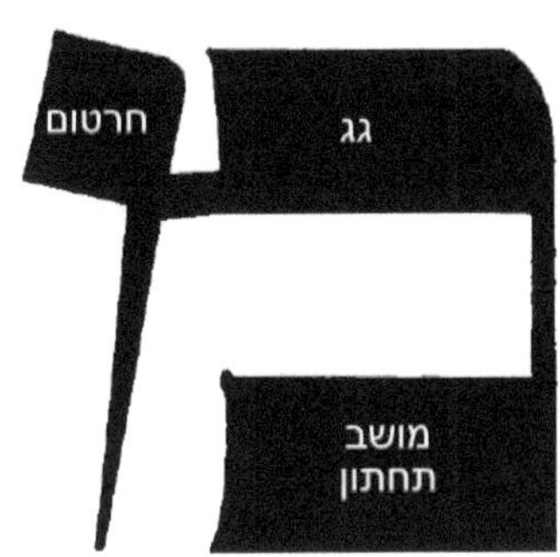

מ' פתוחה ומ"ם סתומה צריכין שיהיו שוים לכתחלה בכל היכולת	The mem petucha and the mem setuma should be לכתחלה similar as much as possible	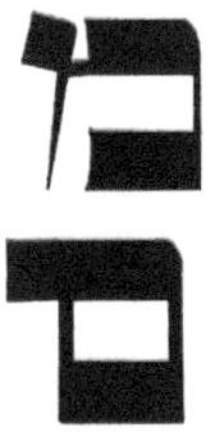
שהרי שתיהן נקראות מ"ם אלא שזו פתוחה וזו סתומה	Both are called mem, except this is open and this is closed	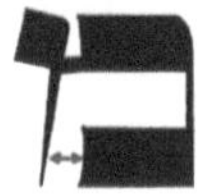
ולכן אין לעשות את המ"ם הפתוחה עגולה למעלה	Therefore the mem petucha should not be round above	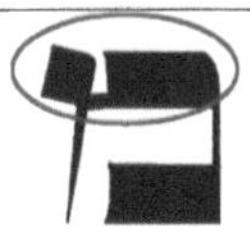
ולמטה בצד ימין	And on the bottom on the right	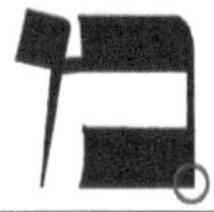
שאם היה עושה כן במ"ם סתומה שמא היתה מתדמית לסמ"ך לתינוק	If one were to do this with a mem setuma it might resemble a samech to a child	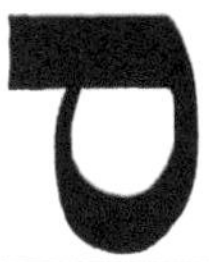
(ועוד כי האותיות צריכים להיות ניכרות מיד כשרואין אותן בראיה	(furthermore because the letters must be recognizable immediately when it is glanced upon	

קלה ולא עד שיסתכל בהן קצת)	and should not require in depth analysis)	
אלא צריך לעשות לה זוית למטה בצד ימין לכתחלה	Rather לכתחלה it must have corners on the bottom on the right side	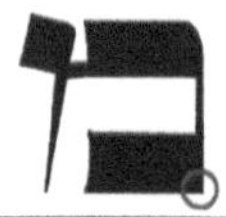
ובלבד שלא יעשה לה שם עקב כמן לבי"ת	As long as there is no עקב as is found on the beis	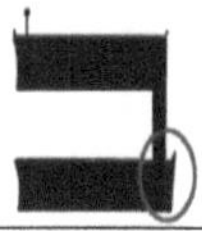
ולמעלה עושין אותה עגולה לכתחלה	Above it should לכתחלה be round	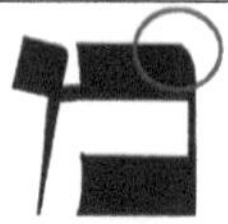
כדי שתהא תמונתה ככא"ף כפופה עם וא"ו	So that it resembles a kaf kefufa with a vuv	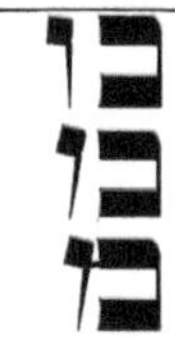
ומטעם זה אין עושין את הגג עגול	And for this reason the גג should not be round	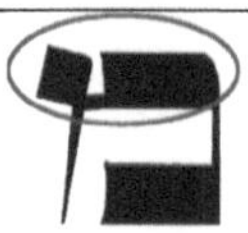
אלא מאריכים אותו בשוה	Rather it should be drawn out equally	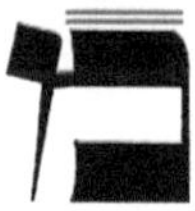
עד כנגד קצה המושב התחתון	Until the end of the base	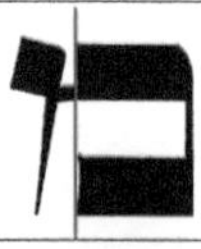
שעל ידי כן דומה לכא"ף כפופה	This way it will resemble a kof kefufa	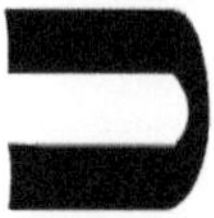
והחרטום צריך שיגיע	And the חרטום should reach	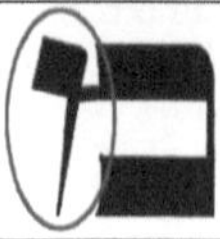

עד כנגד מושב התחתון	Until the base	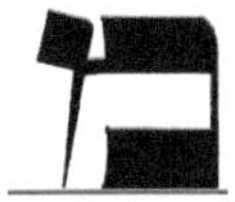
כדי שתהא ראויה לסתום	So that it will be fit to seal	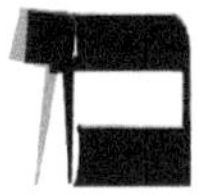
ותמונתה לכתחלה כמו וי"ו עומדת מוטה קצת ולא הרבה	לכתחלה the image is a vuv slight slanted, but not a lot.	
ולכן לא יהיה הפגם שבין הגג ובין ראש החרטום גדול כל כך שיצטרך למשוך ממנה בעקמומית	Therefore the space between the גג and the חרטום should not be so great that the vuv is drawn בעקמומית.	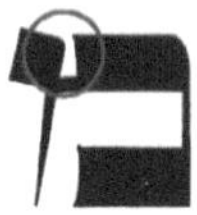

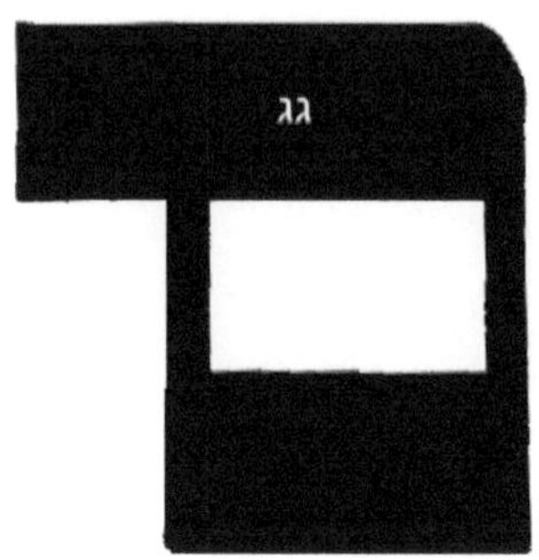

ם' סתומה כבר נתבאר שיש לעשותה למעלה עגולה בצד ימין לכתחלה	The mem setuma was already explained that above it must be round on the right side	
אבל לא למטה	But not on the bottom	
ויש שעושין אותה גם למעלה בצד ימין בזוית	There are those who make the top right also with a corner	
אבל העיקר כסברא הראשונה	However the majority follow the first view	
וגגה יהיה עובר מחוץ לסתימה	And the גג should pass over the area sealed	
כעובי קולמס	The width of a קולמס	קולמס א'

כי זהו שיעור הנקודה של מ"ם פתוחה	This is the measure of the נקודה of the mem petucha	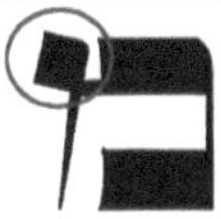
וגם הסתומה תמונתה כא"ף וי"ו	The mem setuma is also a kof and vuv	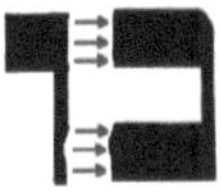
אלא שהוי"ו סותמתה	Except that the vuv seals	
ואם הרחיב צד העליון יותר מן הראוי כזה	And if the upper part is filled more than appropriate as depicted here	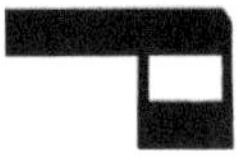
אם אפשר לתקן בקל טוב אבל אם היא בשם קודש תשאר כמו שהיא וכשר	If it is possible to easily correct it should be. If it is in the divine name, it should remain as is and it is kosher.	
(וגם הכא נראה דצריך הבחנת תינוק)	(here too it must be identified by a child)	

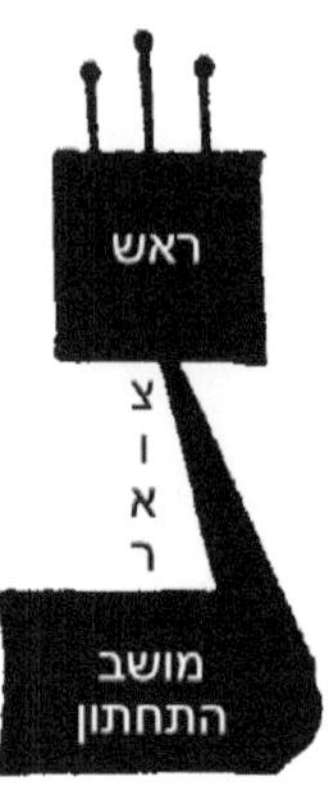

נ' יהא ראשה כמו זיין	The head of the nun is like a zayin	
כי צריכה להיות שוה לנו"ן פשוטה בכל היכולת לכתחלה	Because it must be as similar to the nun peshuta as much as possible	
שהרי שתיהן נקראות נו"ן אלא שזו כפופה וזו פשוטה	Both of them are called nun except that this one is bent and this is straight	
והפשוטה גם כן צריך לעשות בענין שאם תכפפנה תהיה כפופה במשי"ת	The straight one must be made is such a way that if it is doubled over it will be a nun kefufa	
ויהיה הראש קצר	And the head should be short	
ומושבה התחתון משוך לצד שמאל היטב	And the base should be pulled well to the left	
יותר מן הראש	More than the head	

שלא תדמה לבי"ת	So it does not resemble a beis	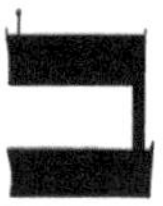
וצוארה קצת ארוך	And the neck in a bit long	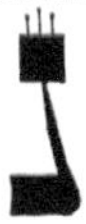
כדי להסמיך אות אצל ראשה	So that another letter can be adjacent to the head	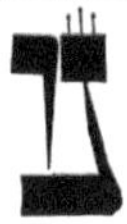
כמ"ש למעלה ותהיה עגולה מלמטה לצד ימין	As written above, the bottom should be round on the right side of the base	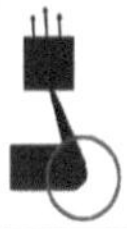
וכן כל האותיות הכפופות צ"ל לכתחלה עגולות למטה	And all the doubled over letters should be round on the bottom	
שאם תפשטנה תהיה פשוטה	Such that if they are straightened out they will resemble the peshuta.	

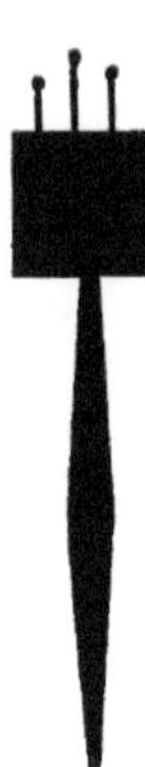

ן' פשוטה צורתה כמו זיי"ן	The nun peshuta is like a zayin	
אך שהיא ארוכה	Except that it is longer	
כשיעור דתהא ראויה להעשות נו"ן כפופה אם תכפפנה כמ"ש למעלה בכא"ף פשוטה	Sufficiently long that a nun can be made if it is doubled over, as was written above by the kof peshuta	
ואם היא קצרה מראין לתינוק ואם קורא זיי"ן פסולה	If it is small it is shown to a child and if the child identifies it as a zayin the writings are invalid	

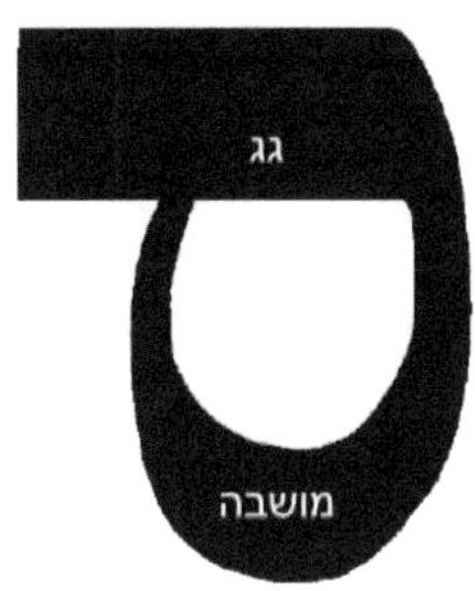

ס' צריכה שתהא מלמעלה גגה שוה לכתחלה	לכתחלה the samech should have a גג which is straight	
כי היא מחוברת משתי אותיות כ"ף כפופה דבוקה אם וא"ו בסופה	Because the samech is the combination of two letters kof kefufa and vuv at the end	
וצריכה שתהיה עגולה בשלש זויותיה	And it must be round on its three corners	
ומושבה קצר	And the base is short	
וגגה למעלה יהא לכתחלה עובר חוץ לסתימה	And the גג should לכתחלה go over the סתימה	

כעובי קולמס	One קולמס measure	
שהוא שיעור ראשה של וא"ו	Because this is the measure of the head of the vuv	

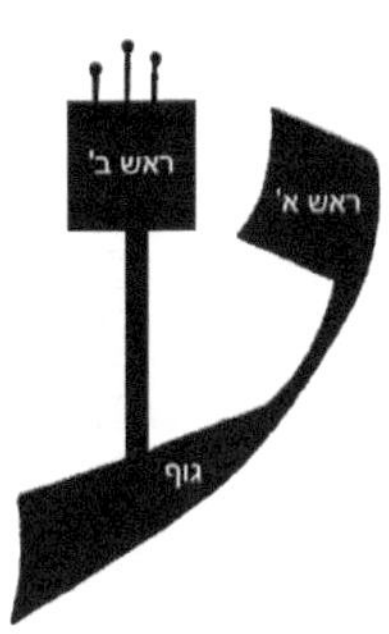

ע' יהיה הראש דראשון	The first head of the ayin	
כעין יו"ד	Should be similar to the yud	
שפניה מעט למעלה מטעם שנתבאר למעלה באות טי"ת	The face should be slightly upwards as explained above in the letter tes	
וגופה בעמידה כדי שיוכל להסמיך אות אצלה	And the body should be standing so that another letter can be placed adjacent to her	
והראש השני יהיה כמו זיי"ן עומד בה מטעם שנתבאר למעלה שם	The second head should be like a zayin standing there as explained above, there	
אבל על פי קבלת האר"י ז"ל יהיה ב' קוין של העייני"ן שבתפילין כמו שתי ווין ישרות	According to the tradition of the Ari Z"L the two lines of the ayin in tefillin should be like two straight vuvs.	

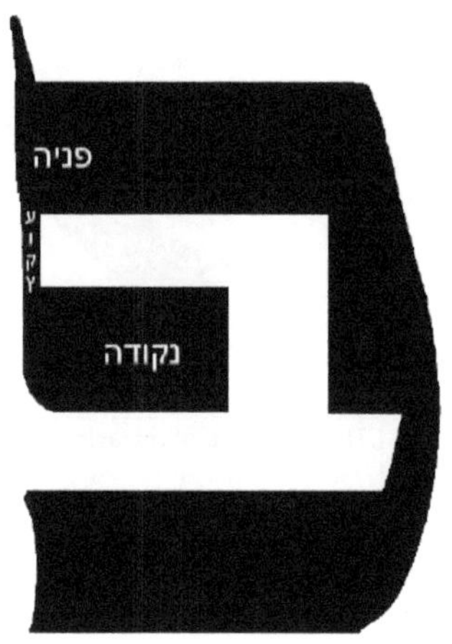

פ' כפופה קבלה מהחסיד לעשות לה זויות לכתחלה למעלה בצד ימין מבפנים	The peh kefufa; there is a tradition from the חסיד to לכתחלה make it corners above on the inner right hand side	
ומבחוץ	And on the outside	
אבל למטה תהיה עגולה מבחוץ כמו כל הכפופות שצריכות להיות עגולה למטה לכתחלה	However, below it should be round on the lower outside	
אבל מבפנים שם תהא לה זויות כדי שיהא בלבן שבפנים צורת ב' כי כן קבלה מהחסיד	But inside it should corners so that the white space will have the shape of the letter beis, for this is the tradition of the חסיד	

ויעשה לה עוקץ על פניה לצד שמאל	And there should be an עוקץ on the left face	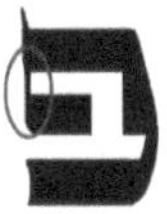
ועוקץ זה ירד למטה אל הנקודה בתוכה	And this עוקץ will go down to the נקודה inside	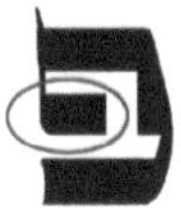
שהנקודה ומשך העוקץ יהיה כמתונת וי"ו	And the נקודה and continuation of the עוקץ should have the image of a vuv	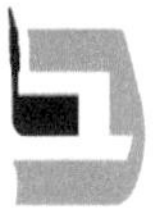
ולכן תהיה הנקודה למטה לצד שמאל עגולה	Therefore the נקודה on the bottom left should be round	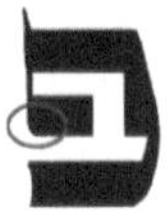
ויזהר שלא תיגע הנקודה אפילו בעוקץ דק בשום מקום	And one should be careful that the נקודה does not touch any other part of the letter	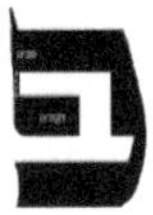
חוץ מן העוקץ שהיא תלויה בו:	Except for the עוקץ from which it is attached.	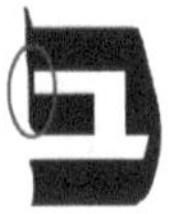

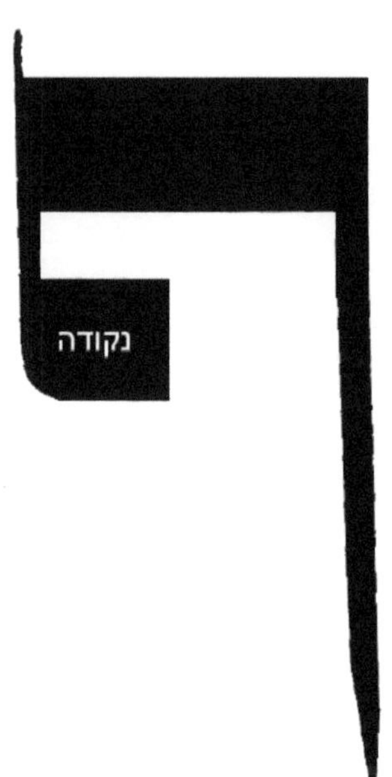

ף' פשוטה צריכה להיות עגולה לצד ימין לכתחילה	The peh peshuta should be לכתחלה round on the right side	
כמו שהכפופה היא למטה	Just like the kefufa is below	
אבל קבלת החסיד לעשותה מרובעת למעלה	However, the tradition of the חסיד is to make it square	

כמו שהכפופה היא למעלה	Just like the kefufa is above	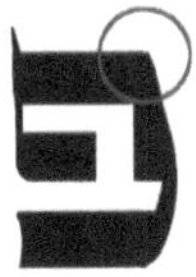
וצריך להיות ארוכה לכתחלה	And לכתחלה it should be long	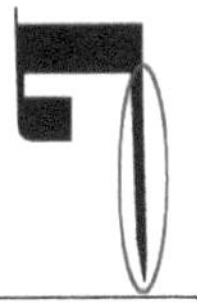
כשיעור שתהא ראויה להעשות פ"א כפופה אם תכפפנה	Sufficiently so that it can be made into a kefufa if it is bent over	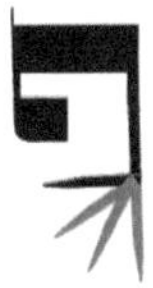
ויזהר בנקודה שבתוכה	And one should be meticulous regarding the נקודה inside	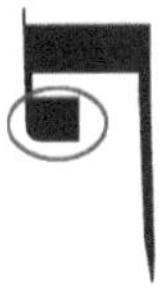
שלא תהא הפוכה לצד חוץ	That it should not be turned outside	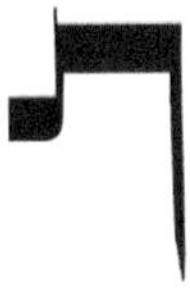
פת דתמה לתי"ו:	Lest it resemble a tav	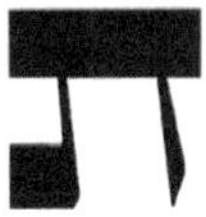

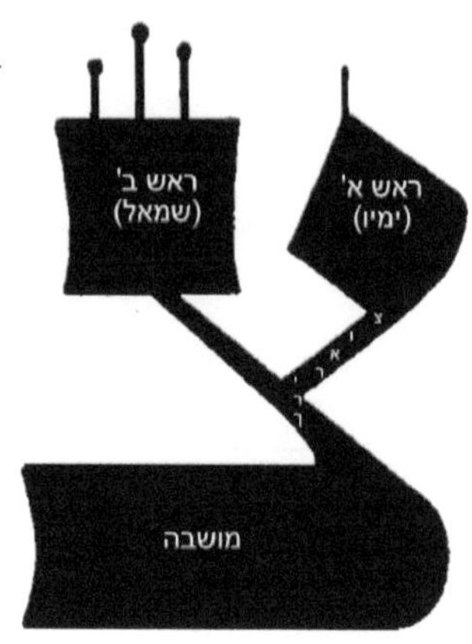

צ' כפופה ראשה הראשון	The first head of the tzadi kefufa	
יהא כפוף קצת כלפי מעלה	Should be bent over, upwards	
מטעם שנתבאר למעלה	For the reasons previously explained	
וירכה ידביק באמצע צוארה	And the ירך should be attached to middle of the neck	
ולא למטה	And not to the bottom	
פן תדמה לעי"ן	Otherwise it will resemble an ayin	

וראשה השני	And the second head	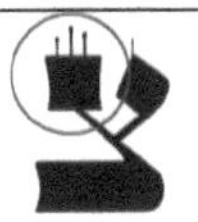
כמו זיי"ן מטעם שנתבאר למעלה	Is like a zayin for reasons explained above	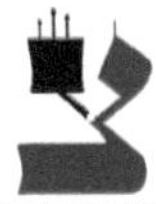
וצוארה קצת ארוך	And the neck is slightly long	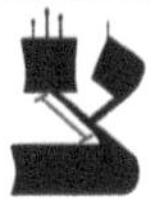
כדי להסמיך אות אצל ראשה	So other letters can be placed next to the head	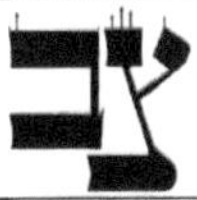
ומושבה	And the base	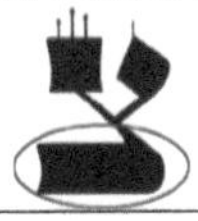
משוך לצד שמאל היטב	Is pulled ot the left	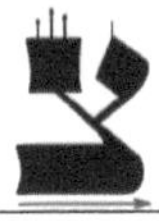
כי תואר גופה היא כמו נו"ן כפופה ויו"ד עליה	The image of its body is a nun kefufa and a yud on it	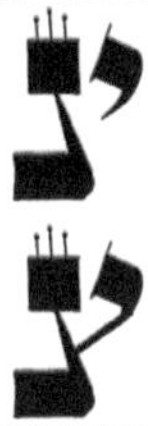
ותהיה עגולה למטה בצד ימין לכתחלה כמו בכל הכפופות	And it should be round on the bottom right לכתחלה, like all the bent over letters	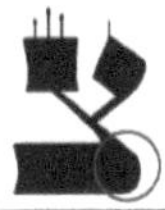
אם כתב יו"ד העליונה הפוכה כזה	If the upper yud was written backawards like this:	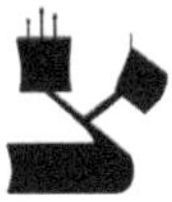
אם אפשר לתקן בנקל יתקן	If it can be easily corrected it should be corrected	
ועפ"י קבלת האר"י ז"ל כל הצדיקי"ן שבתפילין יהיו ראש ימין כמו יו"ד הפוכה	According to the tradition of the Ari Z"L, all the tzadi in tefillin should have the right head like a backward yud	

ושמאל נו"ן כפופה	And the left should be a nun kefufa.	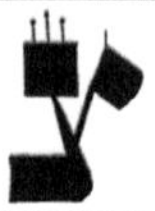

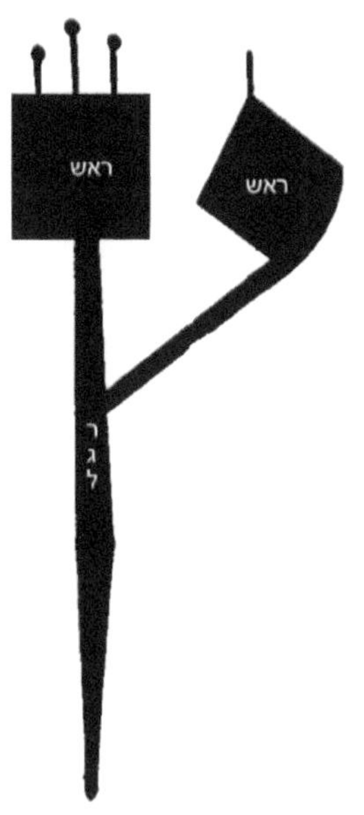

ץ' פשוטה תהינה ראשיה כמו של הכפופה	The first head of the tzadi peshuta should have the same head as the kefufa	
ורגלה	And the foot	
תרד למטה מדיבוק הראשים לכתחלה	Should לכתחלה go down from the place where the heads connect	

בכדי שתהא ראויה לעשותה כפופה	So that there is enough to make it kefufa[17]	

[17] Actually when bent over as can be seen in the picture, the tzadi looks like an ayin and such a letter would likely be invalidated by the reading of a child. However, the idea is the measurement. As noted in the section with the tzadi kefufa, the base is bulled to the left, and the attachment to of the ירך and רגל would have to be a bit higher.

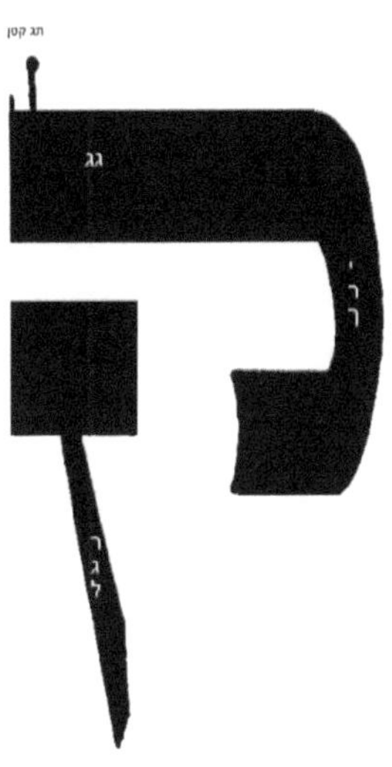

ק' צריך לעשות תג קטן על גגה בצד שמאל	The kuf must have a small תג on the גג on the left side	
נוטה לצד הרי"ש	Slanting towards the reish	
וירכה הימינית	And the right ירך	
צריך להיות עקומה היטב לצד רגל שמאל	Should be slanted to the left foot	

ורגל שמאל	And the left foot	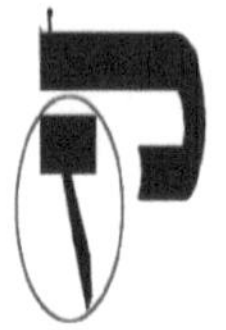
לא יגע לא בירך	should not touch the ירך	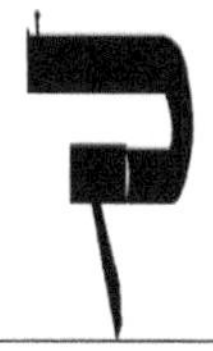
ולא בגג ואם נגע פסול	Nor should it touch the גג and if it touched the writings are פסול	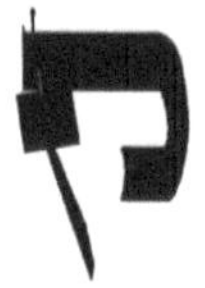
ולא ירחיקו מן הגג הרבה	And it should not be very far from the גג	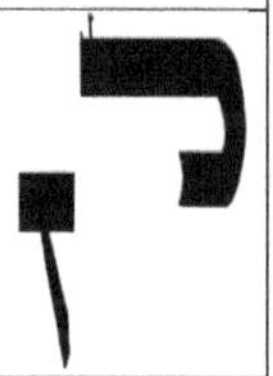
אלא כמו נקודת הה"א	Rather it should be like the נקודה (dot) of the heh	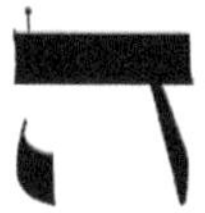
ויש למשוך אותו קצת באלכסון לצד ימין	And it should be extended diagonally slightly towards the right	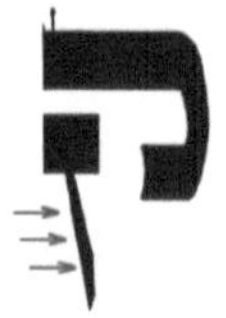
אם משך את הגג יותר מן הראוי והרגל הוא באמצע דינה כמו בה"א	And if the גג was extended more than appropriate such that the foot is in the middle, the laws are like those of the letter heh.	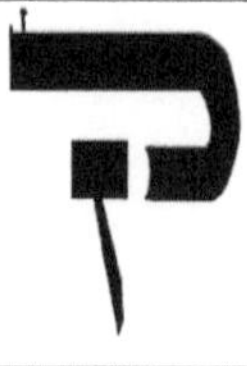

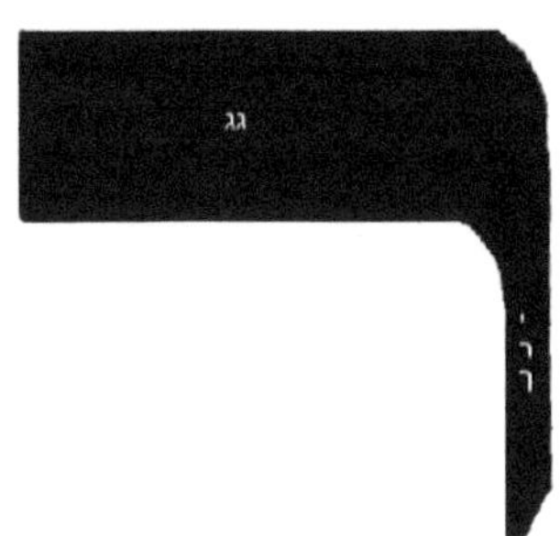

ר' תהיה עגולה ממש למעלה	The reish should be completely round above	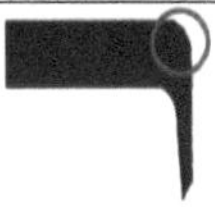
שלא תדמה לדל"ת ותפסול על ידי קריאת התינוק	So that it will not resemble the daled and be invalidated through the reading of a child	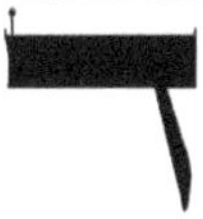
וגגה ארוך	And the גג is long	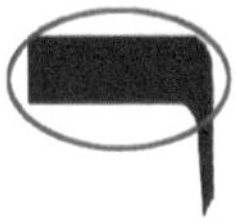
שלא תדמה לוי"ו	So it will not resemble a vuv	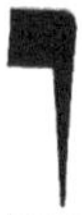
וירכה קצר	And the ירך is short	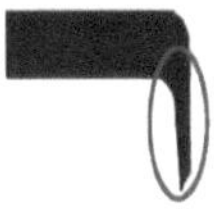
שלא תדמה לכא"ף פשוטה ותפסול על ידי קריאת התינוק:	So it will not resemble a kaf peshuta and be invalidated through the reading of the child	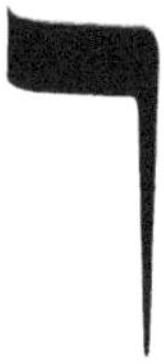

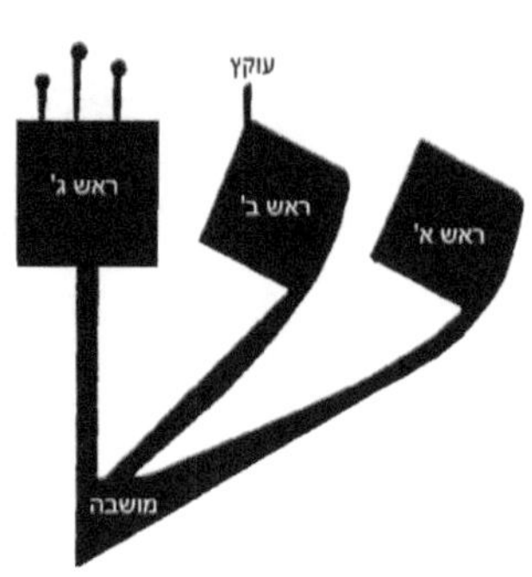

ש' ראשה הראשון כעין יו"ד	The first head of the shin should be like a yud	
שפניה למעלה	That the face is upwards	
וכן ראשה השני מטעם שנתבאר למעלה	And the same with the second head as was explained previously	
הראשון עם גופו	The first with its body	
הוא כעין וי"ו	Is like a vuv	
נמשך בשיפוע עד קצה רגל השלישי	Extended to the extremity of the third leg	

והראש האמצעי	The middle head	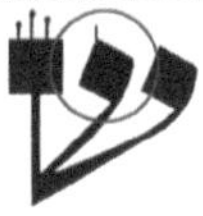
הוא כמו יו"ד	Is like a yud	
ועליה עוקץ משמאל	And it has an עוקץ on the left	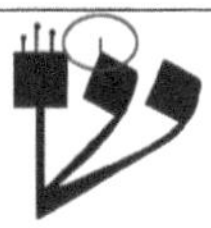
וראש השלישי	And the third head	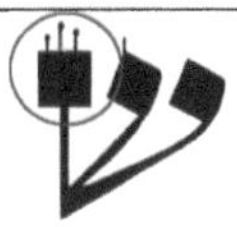
כעין זיי"ן מטעם שנתבאר שם	Is like a zayin as explained previously	
ולפי קבלת האר"י ז"ל כל השיני"ן שבתפילין יהיו ג' קוין	According to the tradition of the Ari Z"L, all the shins in the tefillin should be three lines	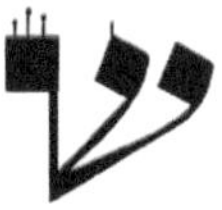
כמו ג' ווי"ן ישרות	Like three straight vuvs	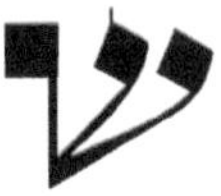
וצריך לדבק ראש האמצעי	And the middle head must be attached	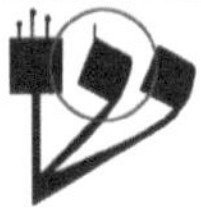
לצד שמאלה למטה	To the left side below	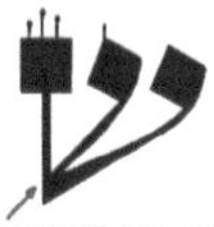
ומושבה למטה	The base on the bottom	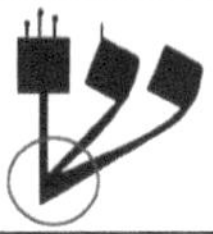

לא יהיה רחב	Should not be wide	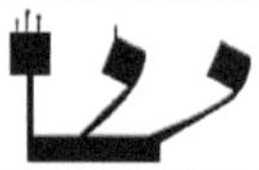
אלא חד לצד שמאל לכתחלה	Rather it should לכתחלה be sharp to the left side	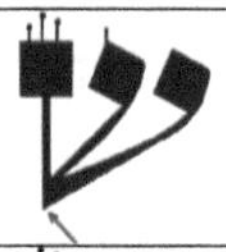
ואז יהיו כל הג' ראשים עומדים למטה על רגל א'	And then all three head will stand on the bottom on one leg	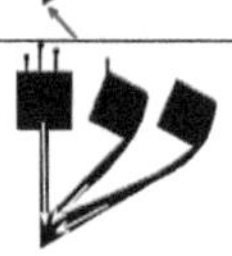
כמו הקו"ף	Like the kuf	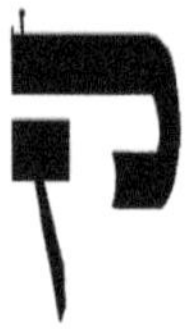
והרי"ש	And the reish.	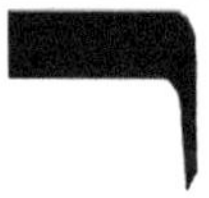

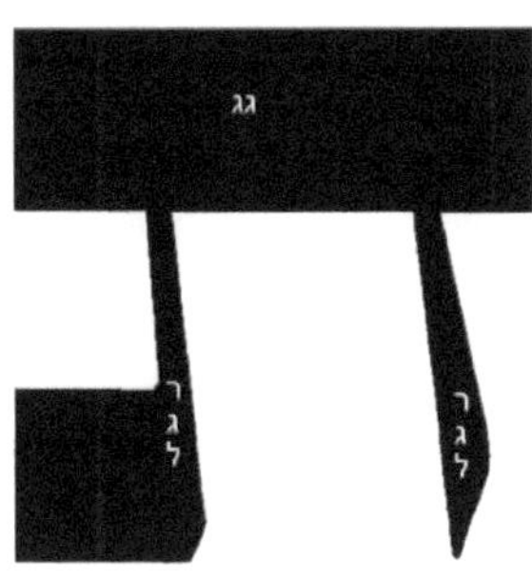

ת' קבלה מהראשונים שיהיה גגה	Regarding the taf, the tradition from the Reishonim is that the גג	
עם רגל הימין	With the right foot	
כמו דל"ת	Should be like a daled	
ורגל שמאל	And the left foot	
יש שעושין כעין וא"ו הפוכה	Some make it like an inverted vuv	
ויש שעושין כמו דל"ת קטנה הפוכה	And some make it like a small inverted daled	
וכל מקום שההלכה רופפת בידך הלך אחר המנהג: וכל זאת לכתחלה	In each place where the halachah is not clear, follow the tradition. This is לכתחלה	
אם משך גג דתא"ו יותר מן הראוי והרגל באמצע	If the גג of the taf was dragged out more than appropriate, and the foot is in the middle	
דינה כמו בה"א וקו"ף:	The laws are like those of a heh and kuf:	

Each letter must be גולם אחד. For example the yud of the ayin, peh, tzadi, shin, the foot of the tuf, they all most have the yud attached, and if not attached the writings are פסול. Similarly, the mem setuma and the samech msut be made in such a way that they are attached completely. Even a small separation, כחוט השערה a hairs breadth, makes them פסול. Similarly, the other letters with the exception of the foot of the heh and the kuf, which are not to be attached, and if they are attached the writings are invalid. A person should be careful with each letter that it should not touch, even itself, even with a thin עוקץ, except from the place where it is to be attached.

4) The letters of שעטנ"ז ג"ץ and the same applies to the nun peshuta and the tzadi kefufa, in every place where they have a zayin with three תגין, they should resemble three small zayins, like a חוט השערה. The תגין should touch the body of the letter, and each תג should be distinct from the other. If they are not attached to the body of the letter, or they touch each other they are invalid and must be corrected. Each תג must distinctly reach the body of the letter, distinct rom the place where it is connected such that it resembles a zayin, not an ayin or shin. They should not be attached to the end of the letter, but rather the middle. בדיעבד if no תגין were made, the writings are כשר. There are those who invalidate any writings without the תגין of שעטנ"ז ג"ץ and one should be stringent according to this view, and correct any writings lacking the תגין. Even by tefillin and mezuzah the correction helps and there is not an issue of writing out of order, since the form of the letter was already there.
5) There is a tradition among the scribes to make special תגים is certain places, and one should not be concerned with this. One should be meticulous that when the תג is made on the yud or vuv that it be very fine, so it does not compromise the form of the letter.
6) There are those who say it is improper to write mundane matters in the כתב אשורית script which is used to write the torah.

ו

The laws of checking via a child
4 Sections

1) Any letter regarding which there is an uncertainty if it was properly formed,[1] is shown to a child. This child should be neither smart nor foolish, and if the child knows to read the letter correctly it is kosher. This is specifically if we are uncertain as to the status of the letter, that it avails to show the letter to the child. The child is then just clarifying what is in front of us.[2] However, if we see that the letter was not formed properly, similarly if the yud from the alef, ayin or shin were detached or the foot of the tuv was detached etc., even though the child can read it correctly, since we see the letter was not formed properly the writings are invalid.

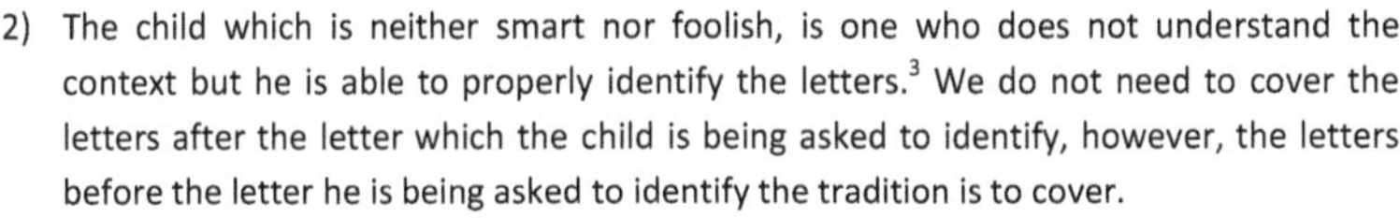

2) The child which is neither smart nor foolish, is one who does not understand the context but he is able to properly identify the letters.[3] We do not need to cover the letters after the letter which the child is being asked to identify, however, the letters before the letter he is being asked to identify the tradition is to cover.

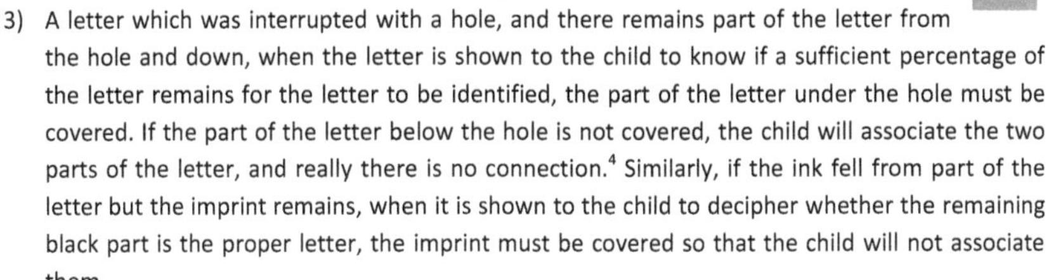

3) A letter which was interrupted with a hole, and there remains part of the letter from the hole and down, when the letter is shown to the child to know if a sufficient percentage of the letter remains for the letter to be identified, the part of the letter under the hole must be covered. If the part of the letter below the hole is not covered, the child will associate the two parts of the letter, and really there is no connection.[4] Similarly, if the ink fell from part of the letter but the imprint remains, when it is shown to the child to decipher whether the remaining black part is the proper letter, the imprint must be covered so that the child will not associate them.
4) If the letter is shown to a few children, and they are not in agreement as to whether the letter is valid, the majority of the children's opinion is followed.

[1] The Kesest Sofer explains that the deformation is such that the letter might not have the correct form and thus would be invalid.
[2] That is the child is not the decider, rather he is clarifying what we presumably already know.
[3] i.e. The child is able to read, but does not understand what he is reading. We don't want the letter to be deciphered based on contextual clues.
[4] Since the hole prevents any connection from existing between the main body of the letter and the part beyond the hole.

That the writings must be clear and the space between letters and words
9 sections

1) The verse states וכתבתם and it is concluded that the writings must be כתיבה תמה clear and simple writings, that each letter must be easily identified. Part of this is that no letter should be attached to another, even with a narrow עוקץ, even the תגין should not touch. Rather each letter should be surrounded by parchment on all sides. If one wrote the alef and the lamed together (as shown to the above right) the writings are not valid.

2) The space between letters should be slight כחוט השערה, a hairsbreadth. The letters should not be separated to a great degree, otherwise one word will appear like two. Between words the space should be the equivalent of a small letter. The words should not be too close together, so that two words do not appear to be one word. If one did not write appropriately, and they made a space between the letters such that one word appeared to be two words, to the child who is neither smart nor foolish, or that two words are so close that the child identifies them as one word, the writings are invalid. If a letter is missing at the end of a word, or at the beginning, and the letter was left hanging above, between the lines, even though if this letter was inserted to the line there would be no space between the two words, the writings are kosher because we now see that they are two words.[5]

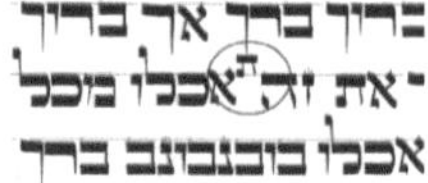

3) The parchment must be complete, without holes. If the hole is small, such that the ink passes over it and seals it, it is kosher. If after the writing, the hole can be discerned when the parchment is held to the sun, if the hole is in a thin line of the letter and it thus divides the letter, it is invalid. However, if it is in a place where the letter is thick, and the ink surrounds the hole on all sides it is kosher (ונ"ל that parchment should be pasted on the outside and the hole should be filled with ink). According to the Keset Sofer, if the ink does not surround the entire hole, even though the letter is not divided in two, for example the whole is at one side of the letter and this causes part of the letter not to be surrounded by parchment, even though the hole is thin, one should be stringent,

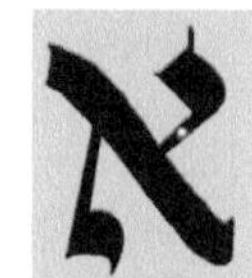

Hole surrounded by ink

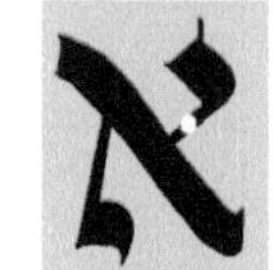

Hole not surrounded by ink

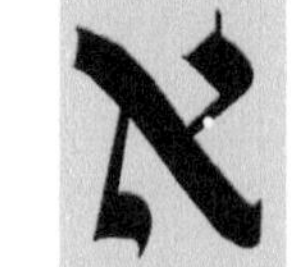

A hole causing the letter not to be surrounded by parchment

[55] It should be noted that the tradition is not to insert these hanging letters.

even if the holes can only be seen when held to the sun.

4) If the רגל foot of the kaf peshuta, or a similar letter, reaches the end of the parchment, whether this is the end of the sheet of parchment or whether there is a hole in the middle of the sheet of parchment, and the letter was extended until the hole, or the hole is on the side of the letter, whether inside or outside, it is invalid, since at the beginning of its writing the letter was not surrounded by parchment.[6]

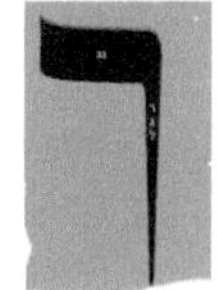

5) The only time that the division of the letter invalidates the letter, is if the division is noticed. However, if there was a thin crack in the parchment, which is only visible when one looks closely, and the crack does not pass through the entire parchment[7] but is only visible from the side of the writings, and the crack is attached and is only noticeable when picked up from the other side of the parchment, it is kosher.

6) If after the letter was written properly, the parchment got a hole and the letter was thus divided, if the amount of letter remaining, aside from the part beyond the hole, is discernible as that letter it is kosher. If not the writings are invalid. If there is uncertainty, for example the leg of the vuv was divided and it is not certain if it still has the shape of a vuv or perhaps a yud, similarly if a nun peshuta was divided and we are not certain if the form of the nun remains, or the form of the zayin etc. a child neither smart or foolish is brought and if he reads the letter properly it is kosher and if not the writings are invalid.

7) The left leg of the heh was punctured; if there remains the measure of a yud, it is kosher. If not the writings are invalid. Similarly, if the right foot of the heh was punctured, if there remains the measure of a yud it is valid, as long as the left leg is aligned with what remains from the right leg. If not this is obviously problematic since there is no longer the shape of the heh. If it was divided in the thick area, if a small line חוט דק like a small vuv וא"ו דקה remains it is kosher.[8]

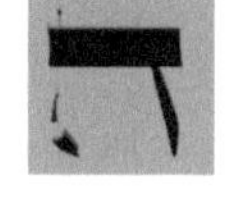

8) If there was a hole in the empty space of the beis or heh etc. even though the entire space was pierces and it is not surrounded with parchment, and similarly if the space between two letters was punctured, and there is no parchment between the letters, the writings are kosher because at the beginning of the writings the letters were surround by parchment. There are those who invalidate in this situation. If possible one should גרור, scrape away, some of the letter so that it will be surrounded by parchment.

9) One must be careful that the head of the lamed of one line should not enter the empty space of a letter above. Even if they are not touching.

---

[6] It will later be discussed what the law is if the letter was written properly surrounded by parchment, and the whole in the parchment developed later.

[7] It can not be seen from the other side of the parchment.

[8] If the hole was made in the קוצה של יו"ד this will be explained in חקירה ד'.

10) If מצות was written with an extra vuv, and the vuv was erased and the tzadik was elongated below, it is proper to be stringent. As long as the letter is not elongated also above, it פנ אר־צנ is considered to be two words. However, if at the beginning of the writing the bottom רגל is elongated and the adjacent letter is written in the letter with the elongated bottom (example is on the right) the writings are permitted because this is one word.

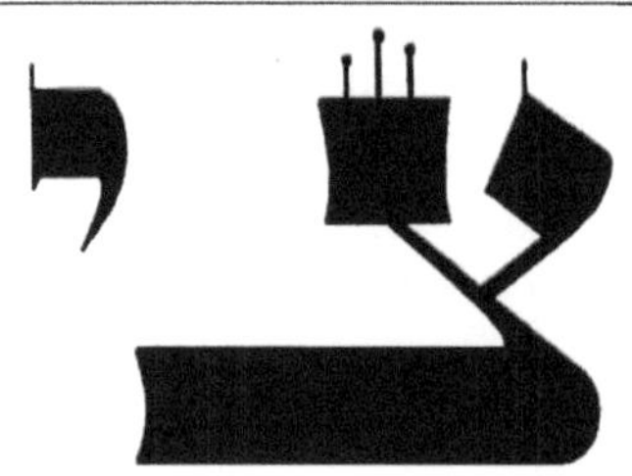	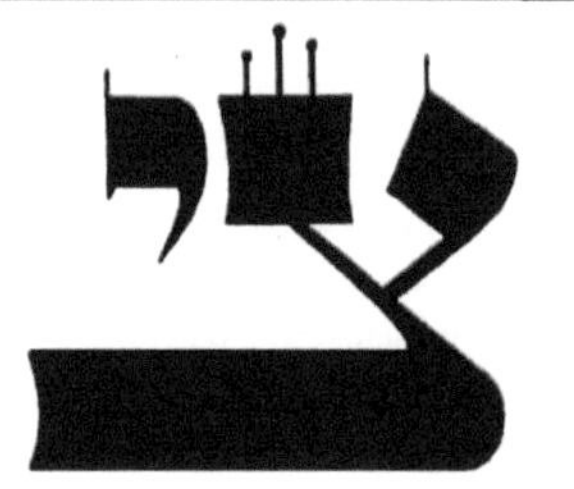
Shown above is a tzadi with an elongated base. The yud is aligned with the end of the base and the writings are not valid.	Shown above is a tzaid with an elongated base. The yud is aligned with the top of tzadi, and is placed without regard for the base of the tzai. This is acceptable.

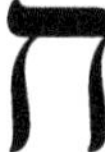

The invalidation of חק תוכות
16 sections

1) We have further learned from the word וכתבתם that the letters must be made specifically through penmanship and not by engraving i.e. not via חק תוכות. For example, if a person scraped out the middle of the letter and its sides, and the resulting carving produce a letter, the writings are not valid because of חק תוכות. Therefore, if a person erroneously wrote a daled in place of a reish or beis in place of a kof (or the other way) the proper method of correction is not to scrape away the תג, for this would be חק תוכות.
2) Even if only part of the letter was created via חק תוכות, the writings are nonetheless invalid. Therefore, if one began and wrote part of the letter properly and it became ruined via a mistake or by a spot of ink falling on the writings, and a bit of the letter is missing, even if only the קוץ is missing, assuming it is a קוץ which invalidates the writings, and the person scraped from the ruined writings, and only via the scraping did the proper form of the letter emerge, this is considered to be חק תוכות and the writings are not valid. If the damage is to be corrected, the entire area must be scraped away, and each letter must be written properly. However, letters which are a combination of two writings[9], and the second writing became invalid, only the part which became invalid needs to be scraped away.[10] The scribes must be meticulous in the laws of חק תוכות. Some of which ware explained here, from these the rest can be deduced.
3) If the top yud of the alef is attached to the middle line which goes by diagonal down the middle, there are two ways this happened. One possibility is that the yud was written first, then the middle line. In this case the yud was written properly and only the middle line must be completely erased, since the middle line was invalidated before it was completed. However, if the middle line was written first and then the yud was written, and it was inappropriately attached, the yud should be erased and not the middle line. The middle line was written properly, and in this case the yud was not written correctly. If the writings were not corrected until the bottom yud was written, then the bottom yud must also be erased. This is the rule: anything written when the letter was invalidated must be

א

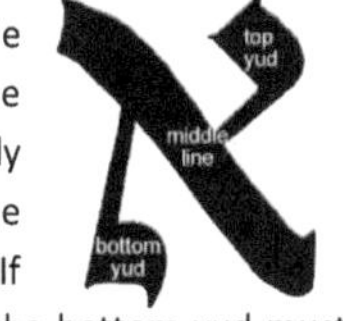

[9] The language used by the Kesset Sofer is one of כתיבה, however, by the word writings what is really meant is strokes. Some letters are created by two writings, means that the letter is created by two strokes.
[10] The implication here is only the invalid stroke must be undone. If a letter was composed of two strokes, one was valid and the second stroke was not, only the second stroke must be undone.

scratched away. If the bottom yud was improperly attached and not the top yud, then only the bottom yud must be erased and rewritten.

4) If the entire alef was written properly, and ink subsequently fell on the alef, even on the top yud, it is enough to only scrape away that and rewrite it properly.

5) If a drop of ink fell into the open space of the beis, even if the ink is still moist, and the beis now looks like a peah, or the beis no longer looks like a beis, or the ink fell on another letter which is no longer discernible, the writings are not valid. The writings can not be corrected by scraping away the drops of ink until the letter is proper, rather the entire letter must be scratched away. If one erroneously wrote a heh instead of a daled, it is not sufficient to scrape away the foot and the daled will remain. However, the person does not need to scratch away the entire letter. Rather, after the drop is scratched away and the גג is also scratched away, until the form of the daled has been compromised, then it should be completed. If one wrote a kaf peshuta, instead of a heh, the foot of the heh should be erased first until the letter resembles a daled and then the left leg should be written. If the left leg was written first, the entire leg must be erased. If this happened in the writing of the divine name, a rabbinical authority should be consulted.

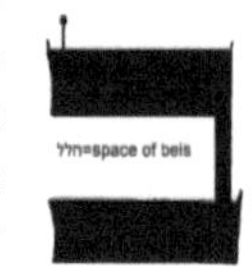

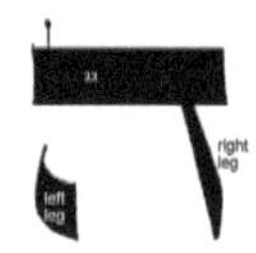

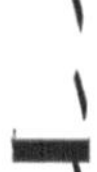

6) A mem petucha in which the opening was attached, and the mem is now sealed, erasing the attachment is not sufficient.[11] Rather the entire חרטום must be erased and it should resemble a kof or a nun kefufa and then it should be completed properly. This is the rule for all letters, which are written in two strokes and became invalidated in one of the strokes, only that stroke which was invalidated must be scratched away. However, a reish which was made to resemble a daled, one should be stringent. It would not be sufficient to erase the ירך and rewrite it as a reish, because both the גג and the ירך were not made properly. Rather, both must be erased. If the letter was originally written as a reish and then one made a mistake added a תג and it now resembles a daled, it is sufficient to erase the גג or the ירך with the תג and then rewrite the letter as a proper reish. One who is stringent in this regard will be blessed.

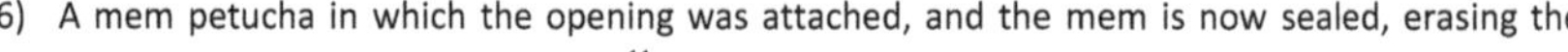

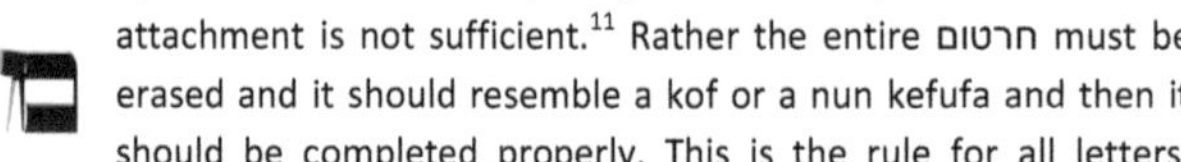

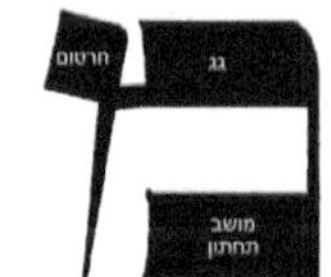

7) The yud which has a left עוקץ which is as long as the right רגל, and it thus resembles a ches, this is the manner by which it is corrected. If the scribe first wrote the yud with the right רגל and then the עוקץ was subsequently added, and elongated more than appropriate, then only the עוקץ and the right רגל must be erased, they should then be written properly. However, if the left עוקץ was made first (as is the tradition of many scribes when writing the yud they make the line thin so there will be the תג and the left עוקץ and from this

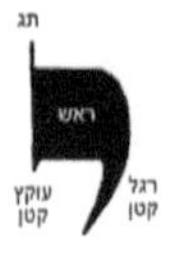

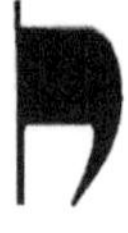

[11] I.e. it is not sufficient to just erase the part of the חרטום which is causing the mem petucha to be sealed but rather as will be explained, the entire חרטום must be erased.

they draw out the rest of the form of the letter yud) then the entire yud must be erased and rewritten anew. If it can be corrected with ink, this is better.[12]

8) Some of the greatest authorities ruled that even a letter which was written in two strokes, like a mem petucha which was sealed etc. it is not sufficient to scrape away only the second part which is invalid. Rather, the entire letter must be erased and written anew. When possible, a person should be stringent in this regard לכתחלה.

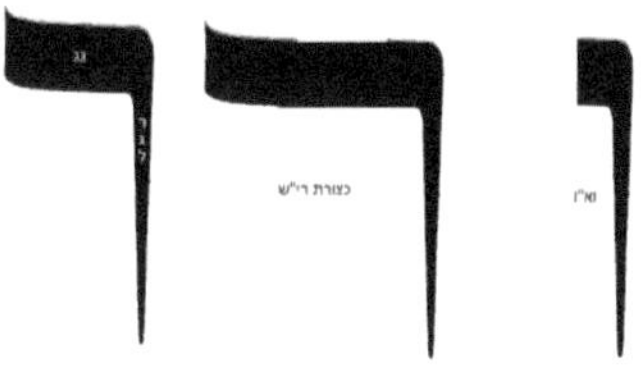

9) If the גג of the kof peshuta was drawn out, such that it resembles a reish, the גג must be scraped away until only the form the vuv remains. If this happened in the name of א-לקיך then see 12:13.

10) If one erroneously wrote a heh instead of a ches, it is preferable to scrape away the entire heh. בדיעבד if it was corrected thus: that the foot and the גג was scraped away until only a bit of the right רגל remained, such that it resembled the letter vuv or zayin, and then from the left side he wrote a zayin and attached them with a חטוטרת, this too would be kosher. Since בדיעבד we permit a ches without the חטוטרת, when the daled of the heh was written, the writing was not invalid since it was possible to form this initial daled into a ches peshuta. Since the daled's writing was not invalid it is not obligatory to erase the entire letter, rather just that which needs to be corrected.

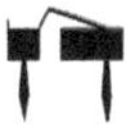

11) If the ches was made thus: that daled and zayin were written then a חטוטרת was placed on top of them. If the scribe attached the end of the right part of the חטוטרת on the right side of the daled, that it is opposite the right רגל like thus,[13] this should be corrected by erasing the daled until it is made into a zayin and it is kosher even in tefillin and mezzahs, even after one wrote subsequent letters (and it is not an issue of writing out of order because this is not corrected by writing). However, if the חטוטרת was attached on the left side of the daled like this,[14] the whole letter or at least the חטוטרת and the גג of the daled must be erased, until only a zayin remains and then the חטוטרת must be rewritten. By tefillin and mezuzahs if one had written subsequent letter, the writings can not be corrected and there is no difference in this regard if the daled was made from the right and the zayin was made from the left side, or the reverse.

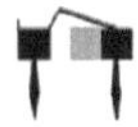

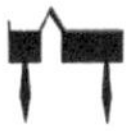

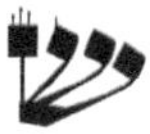

12) If the shin was written with four heads, even though the child identifies the letter as a shin, it cannot be corrected simply by scraping away one yud, so three heads remain. Rather, the form of the shin must be compromised and then rewritten. Otherwise it is חק תוכות. By tefillin and mezuzahs, if subsequent letters were written, there is no method of correction because the writings would then be out of order.

13) In every situation in which a letter became invalidated because of חק תוכות, even if a letter was then passed over the letter, it is to no avail.[15]

---

[12] Corrected with ink means that the letter can be corrected by adding more ink.
[13] This is the letter as published in the Keset Sofer. A clearer rendition is on the right side.
[14] This is the letter as published in the Keset Sofer. A clearer rendition is on the right side.
[15] i.e. The letter is not considered to be written, but rather it was considered to have been חק תוכות.

14) If wax or fats dripped on the letters, even though the letters can not be seen, once the wax and fats are removed, the writings are kosher. This would not be a violation of חק תוכות. Even when the wax or fats were on the letters, the letters were not invalid, they were just covered.

15) If one letter was attached to another letter, but each letter retained its form, if the attachment happened before the completion of the writing of the letter, it is not sufficient to scrape away the connection, unless it is urgent such as the writing of the divine name. According to the Keset Sofer, the same applies to tefillin and mezuzahs if subsequent letters were written, and one must be able to fix the writings.[16] However, if the case is not urgent, then one should scrape away the entire second letter that was attached. However, if the attachment happened after the letters were written. For example, one wrote a vuv adjacent to a nun, and the vuv was attached below to the nun, it is permissible to scrape away only the connection, and this would not be a violation of חק תוכות since the form of the vuv was completed before it was attached. One who is stringent in this regard, to scrape away the entire vuv will be blessed.

16) If after he removed his hand and lifted the quill from the letter, and then two letters became attached, whether it became attached below or above, the attachment is scraped away and there is no problem, as long as the form of the letter was not compromised. If the shape of the letter was compromised by the attachment, whether the first letter or the second letter, it is obvious that the scraping is not sufficient and the writings must be corrected as described above.

[16] Otherwise they would need to be put in גניזה.

9 Tefillin and Mezuzahs must be written in the proper order
11 sections

1) Tefillin and mezuzahs must be written in order, and if they were written out of order, whether the later paragraph was written first or the words or letters were not written in order, the writings are invalid. Therefore, if it was discovered that the one letter was missing from the writings, they can not be corrected unless it possible to scrape away the writings to the place of the missing letter and then write the missing letter and rewrite everything which was scraped away.
2) However, if there is an extra letter this can be corrected by scraping away the extra letter if it is a letter at the end or beginning of a word. However, if the extra letter is in the middle of a word, it can not be corrected because when scraped away the word will appear as two words. If it is possible to stretch out the letter which is before the letter which is to be scraped way, for example if the word לאבותיך was written מלא וא"ו with an extra vuv, the vuv can be erased and the beis can be elongated, this is sufficient. Similarly, if one can widen the letter before or after the letter which must be scraped away this is avails, because it is not changed the letter.
3) Any letter which was written improperly or the form became compromised after it was written, and the letter no longer retains its form, for example if the foot of the alef is attached to the גג of the alef or the face פני האלוף is attached to the גג under it,[17] or the foot heh or kuf are touching (for in all these cases, scraping alone is not sufficient but rather the form of the letter must be compromised and the letter must then be rewriten so it will not be חק תוכות) or the letter was split to two letters, whether this happened at the beginning of the writings or after the completions of the writing, for example a tzadi which became a yud nun, a shin that became an ayin yud, a mem petucha which became kof and vuv. Similarly, a lamed which had an interruption it it's neck and looks like a kof and a vuv. Similarly, a ches written בכתב ספרדית which is without a חטוטרת, if the left foot is split from the גג and appears like a heh, and all similar cases that the split in the ink causes the letters to look like other letters, even if the child reads them properly, if the letters were corrected after subsequent letters had been written, the writings are considered to be שלא כסדרן, out of order and the writings are invalid.
4) If the form of the letter is recognizeable, even if there is a slight interruption, for example; parts of the yuds of alefs, shins, ayins or the feet of the tovs, in the attachment but they are recognized by a child, similarly a beis or daled which were separated פירוד דק from the גג, even though all of these are invalid prior to being corrected, מ"מ they can be corrected even after subsequent writings, since the form of the letter was recognizeable and there is not a problem of writing out of order שלא כסדרן. וה"ה similarly if the חטוטרת of the ches are not touching above, but there separation is not immediately recognizable ניכר להדיא, even though the child will identify this as two zayins, it is permissible to attach them even after subsequent letters were written. The reason the child does not identify this as a ches is because he is not familiar with this ches. Some are concerned in all these scenarios because of שלכם. Even though we are

[17] This might actually be clearer in the Hebrew: כגון נגע רגל האלו"ף בגג האלוף או פני האלוף בפניה בגג שתחתיה

lenient, מ"מ the scribe should be meticulous at the time of the writing that he not need these leniencies. According to the Keset Sofer if the mem setuma or the samech were slightly detached, even if the child reads it appropriately, they should not be permitted to be attached with tefillin and mezuzah, after subsequent letters were written, because of the concern שלא כסדרן that the letters were not written in order.

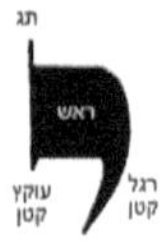

5) It was already noted that the yud must have a תג above on the left side, and an עוקץ below, and the רגל of the right side. If a yud was found lacking the right רגל in the tefillin or mezuah, it can not be corrected. Without this רגל the letter is not called a yud, and when the yud was corrected the writings would be considered שלא כסדרן, written out of order. However, if the left עוקץ is missing, it can be corrected because without this עוקץ the letter is still considered to be a yud. ומ"מ the scribe should be careful to make the עוקץ before subsequent letters are written. Some of the great גדולים opine that the lack of the עוקץ compromises the form of the letter, and it can not be corrected because of שלכם. Even though we are lenient,לכתחלה one should be careful. The same is with the upper תג.

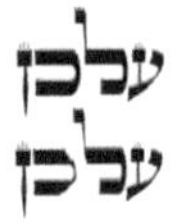

6) Regarding letters which were attached it was already explained that as long as the letter's form was not compromised, the letters can be separated. According to the Keset Sofer, כל שכן the same would apply if two words were adjacent to each other and resembled one word, for example עלכן (see right) if it possible to scrape away part of the lamed and part of the kof so that each of the two words is distinct, this is ideal.

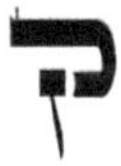

7) If one wrote an extra word, it should be erased. We do not follow the view of the Rabbanu Tam that the הפסק סתימה is three letters. In chapter 11 it will be explained that one should erase the second word. However, if before the first word there is daled, reish, beis or another letter which can be extended, erase the first word so that the writings will also be in compliance with the view of Rabbanu Tam. If once the word is erased there will remain an empty space equal to nine letters, which is a פרשה according to all, it will invalidate the writings. The letters in front of the erasure, if at all possible, should be drawn out. Even if the letter is a heh or kuf, that if drawn out the רגל will not be placed at the end of the letter, one should not be concerned for there is no other option. If the רגל is erased and written at the end of the letter there will be a problem of שלא כסדרן, writing out of order. If there is an alternative this kind of heh of kuf should not be permitted.

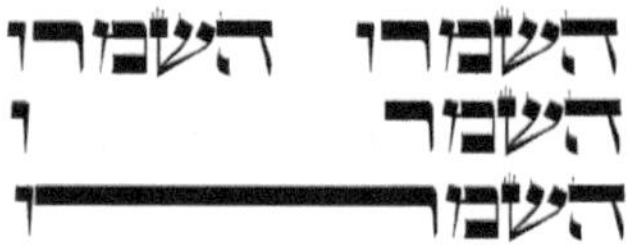

8) If the word השמרו was written twice, it is permissible to erase the vuv from the first השמרו and והשמר from the second השמרו and the last vuv will remain in place and the reish will be extended to the vuv, so that it will be one word. The same in similar cases. Even if the second word, is not in tefillin or mezuzah it is permitted. The rule is that as long as the form of the letter remains, even if it became invalid from the side, it can be elongated to render it kosher and it would not be a problem of שלא כסדרן, writing out of order.

9) A letter of which the ink lost some of its luster, if it is still properly black, more ink can be applied and there is no problem of שלא כסדרן writing out of order. Since the letter is kosher now, the only purpose of the additional ink is to prevent further deterioration. However, if the ink became red or it changed to another color, a color other than black, the application of additional black ink would be of no avail and the writings would thus be considered שלא כסדרן out of order.
10) Since the tefillin and mezuzahs must be writing כסדרן in the proper order, one must be careful when they write the divine name (which can not be erased) that all which was previously written should be read carefully, so that the parchment will not need to be put in גניזה. Similarly, each chapter of the tefillin, after it was written it should be read well with meticulous concentration, two or three times. Perhaps there is something invalid in the writings and it will thus invalidate the subsequent writings. One must be careful that this does not happen.
11) We do not hang letters in tefillin or mezuzahs even if the writings are כסדרן, in the proper order. For example if a person needed to write מימים ימימה and he saw there was not room and he hung the word ימים above between the lines and then below between the lines he wrote ימימה the writing are not valid.

10 The holiness of the divine name and its writing
18 sections

1) Even though the person said at the beginning of the writing that the writings will be לשם קדושת ספר תורה for the holiness of the sefer torah, tefillin or mezuzahs, each time he comes to write one of the divine names, which are holy, pure, and can not be erased, he must sanctify the writings prior to the writing. Even part of the divine name which he wants to write, for example if he compromised a letter or part of a letter such as the קוץ of the yud which invalidates if compromised, and he wants to repair it, he must sanctify the writings from the beginning.
2) Therefore, if a letter is missing from the divine name, or from one of the words adjacent to the divine name is a letter from which a letter can be used to complete the divine name, even if these letters were נטפלין (they are not sanctified in their own right), for example the scribe needed to write אלקים and he erred and though that he had to write אלקינו, and when he realized his mistake he wanted to make the nun into a mem setuma, this is forbidden, since the nun and vuv were not sanctified.
3) How are the writings sanctified? Prior to the writing the scribe will utter הנני כותב לשם קדושת השם "behold I am writing for sake of the holiness of the name," some say the words do not need to be uttered rather it is sufficient that he will think that he is writing for the divine name בדיעבד the lenient view can be relied on.
4) If there was not even a thought מחשבה that the writings should be for the divine name, the writings are invalid. Since the writings are invalid, passing the quill over the writings are applying additional ink is of no avail as far as the sanctity of the letters. Even if there is one name which the scribe forgot to sanctify, and he does not know which one, the entire sefer torah would be invalid.
5) If one was writing two or three divine names, לכתחלה each divine name should be sanctified on its own. For each one is its own name and requires its own concentration. בדיעבד it is sufficient to have one sanctification for all the names, if there was no pause between writing each of the divine names.
6) Just as one is obligated to sanctify the great and exalted name השם הנכבד והנורא so to the person is forbidden to sanctify names which are not holy such as לא יהיה לך אלהים אחרים.[18] Even a name which is not referring to עכו"ם only on something else such as עד האלהים יבא דבר שניהם which is explained as referring to judges. Similarly, יש לאל ידי and similar cases the divine names may not be sanctified for the holy name, may It be blessed. Since these words are mundane and not worthy of sanctity, it is similar to sanctifying blemished animals for the alter.
7) There are many names in the torah, which according to the simply understanding it is unclear if they are divine or mundane. One must do as was decided by our rabbis or blessed memory. There are names that even the rabbis of blessed memory did not conclude if they are holy or mundane and their status is still uncertain. These names must be sanctified conditionally that is

---

[18] This is the prohibition of idolatry and the word אלהים is referring to an idol. As noted, it must not be sanctified.

at the time of the writing the scribe will verbally stipulate הנני כותב לשם קדושת השם אם הוא קודש "I am writing for the holiness of the name if it is holy."

8) If the scribe is writing the divine name and he know it is the name of הקב"ה but he forgot to sanctify it at the beginning of the writings but he realized his error before he completed the writing of the divine name, according to the Keset Sofer, the scribe can stil sanctify the name before it was completed. However, if the scribe started writing and he was unaware what he was writing was holy, then it can not be subsequently sanctified.
9) When the scribe is writing and sees that he is close to the divine name, and the ink has almost been exhausted from the quill, and the scribe must dip the quill in the ink well to replenish the quill to write the divine name, the scribe should not write until the divine name, but rather at least a letter before the divine name should remain, the scribe should replenish the ink in the quill and then write this letter and then the divine name. A scribe should not write the divine name immediately after replenishing the ink on the quill, because sometimes there is excessive ink or hair and the writings are not properly. Also because it is necessary to sanctify the ink on the quill prior to writing the divine name. If even one letter does not remain to be written prior to the divine name, and the quill was replenished in the ink well, the person should seek a different letter or תג that need additional ink and this letter or תג should first be completed and then the divine name should be written. However, to write a mundane letter on something else is forbidden because the ink was prepared for the divine name it should not לכתחלה used for mundane writings.
10) If in the midst of the writing of the divine name, the quill ran dry, it should be dipped in the letters before the divine name, if they are still wet, and that ink should be used to complete the divine name.
11) Prior to writing the divine name הנכבד והנורא the scribe must prepare his hear, if he must spit or clear his nose he should do this prior to writing the divine name, and then he should clean his hands. The scribe should sanctify the divine name and write it with clear and pure concentration. The scribe should not pause while writing the divine name. Even if the king of the Jews greets him, he should not respond. ומ"מ if the scribe paused and replied as long as he did not interrupt his concentration the writings are kosher בדיעבד.
12) If the scribe was writing two or three divine names, it is permissible to pause between the writings of each name and to greet anyone. When he returns to his writings he msut sanctify anew the divine name that he intends to write. However, the scribe should not spit even between the writing of the two divine names.[19]
13) The letters of the divine name must be written in order כסדרן even in a sefer torah. However, בדיעבד, if there was a mistake with the first letter and another letter must be written in its place, according to the Keset Sofer this would be permitted in the writing of a sefer torah.
14) If the scribe forgot to write the divine name, the divine name may be hung between the lines. However, it is forbidden to have part of the divine name on the line and part of the divine name

[19] i.e. The scribe should not after completing the writing of one divine name, split before writing the second divine name.

hanging between the lines. והנטפל to the divine name at the end, there is room בדיעבד to be lenient and be lenient if these letters were left hanging.

15) It is permissible to write the name on the plase of erasure (meaning that the letter were erased while the ink was still wet, or the ink dried and the ink was erased with water etc.) and on the place where the writings were scraped way (meaning that the letters were scraped away when the ink dried) and scraping is preferable to erasure.[20]
16) The letters of the divine name and הנטפלין לאחריו, לכתחלה should all be written on the דף and should not go outside the דף. However, בדיעבד it is kosher.
17) There are those who have the הדר not to write the divine name at the end of the column. If it is easy for him, the scribe should do this. However, letters should not be elongated or forced to accomplish this. It is preferable that the divine name should be at the end than to force or to enlarge the letters.
18) There are some scribes who are meticulous not to write the divine name without purifying their own name. This is proper. To accomplish this and entire יריעה will be written and the place of the divine names will be left to be written later after the body was purified. This too is proper. However, to do this in the entire sefer torah there is concern that all the writings will be old and the divine names will be in new ink it will seem like מנומר. This is not proper.

[20] The Lishkat Sofer explains that according to the Shach it is preferable to write the divine name on the place a letter was scraped or erased, rather than to write the divine name hanging between the lines. The Birchei Yosef quotes the Rambam that it is better to hand the divine name between the lines. The Lishkat Sofer concludes that now the tradition is not to hang any letters between the lines, and certainly the divine name should not be written hanging between the lines.

11 The Prohibition of Erasing the Divine Name
18 sections

1) Regarding the עכו"ם it is written ואבדתם את שמם מן המקום ההוא "and thou shall destroy their name from that place" and it is subsequently written לא תעשון כן לה' אלקיכם "do not do this to Hashem thy God." The rabbis of blessed memory said that this is the prohibition of erasing the divine name. If he erases even one letter from the holy and pure names by which הקב"ה is referred, he is violating a biblical prohibition and he is liable for lashes. If part of the divine name was erased on its own, or accidentally by a person, or even on purpose, it is forbidden to erase the rest of the divine name.
2) Even a divine name which was written accidently, if was written in the wrong place, even if it was not written for holy purposes, even if the divine name was created via חק תוכות which is not writing regarding the sefer torah, tefillin and mezuzah, even if the divine name was not written in אשורית but rather is some other script, even if the divine name was created via אריגה , תפירה or מיני צבעונים or any method on any material, all that was made with the intention of the divine name, that is that the one who writes or creates it knows that this is the name of הקב"ה, anyone who compromises even one letter violates the biblical prohibition and is liable for lashes.
3) Even if one does not compromise a latter in the divine name, but rather excises a full letter from the divine name, this too is erasure since it causes the divine name to be lacking.
4) Even a small dot is forbidden to erase from the divine name. Therefore a nun of kof peshuta attached to another letter from the divine name written under it, when the scribe scrapes away the רגל to separate them, he must be careful that the knife should not touch the last part of the attachment. Rather he should leave something, to make sure he does not erase the divine name. If wax or fat dripped on the divine name, they should not be removed with the fingernail, lest the person peel away part of the divine name. Rather, the parchment should be heated from the outside opposite the drop, and it should be removed without any of the writings.

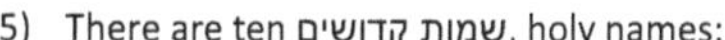

5) There are ten שמות קדושים, holy names:
   a. שם הויה
   b. שם אדנות
   c. אל
   d. אלוה
   e. אלהי
   f. אלהים
   g. שדי
   h. צבאות
   i. יה
   j. אהיה

The rest of the כינויין by which הקב"ה is praised, such as הגדול הגבור והנורא הנאמן האדי וחזק האמיץ העיזוז חנון ורחום קנא ארך אפים ורב חסד are the same as other holy writings and they may be erased if the text needs to be corrected. These are not the names of הקב"ה but rather names of His actions.

6) If one wrote the אל or אלהים or the יה from the name הויה, the letters may not be erased since these are divine names in their own right. However, if someone wrote שד from שדי or צב from צבאות, they can be erased. And this is not specific to צב, rather as long as the divine name has not been completely written it can be erased. There are those who maintain that the אד of אדני, and the אה of אהיה can be erased and those who maintain the letters can not be erased. It is proper to be stringent. The name written in the siddurs with two yuds with a vuv on top,[21] this can be erased if there is great need.
7) The letters הנטפלות להשמות in front of the divine name such as the lamed of לה', the kof of כה', may be erased. However, the letter הנטפלות להשמות which are found after the divine name such as the kof peshuta of אלקיך or the כ"ם if אלקיכם can not be erased since at the time of their writing they were already sanctified by the divine name. Even if these letters have no relevance in this place, if one was to write אלקים and they wrote אלקיך or they had to write אלקיהם and he wrote אלקיכם, even though here they have no relevance to the divine name here, the divine name sanctified them and they may not be erased. However, if one wrote a letter which in no place is connected to a divine name such as a ק or a פ etc. this is not considered נטפל להשם and they can be erased.
8) לקדור (i.e. to cut) the divine name from the parchment complete with the קלף (parchment) the greatest of the Reishonim of blessed memory forbade this because it is not respectful to the divine name. It was ruled that if there is an extra divine name (טעות יתרון) to put the entire parchment in גניזה. Now in many places the tradition of the scribes is that if there is a טעות יתרון, whether the divine name was erroneously written twice or the divine name was written in the wrong place, the divine name along with some letters or the entire verse is cut from the parchment. Another piece מטלית is placed under the hold and that which is lacking is written on this other piece מטלית. These scribes have on what to rely. However, if the divine name is not extra, rather the intention is to escise the area because of another mistake, for example the person forgot other words and wants to add these words between writings of the divine name, and it is impossible to add these words without excising the divine name, to excise these divine names is ודאי אסור prohibited. In places where there is not tradition, an extra divine name should also no be cut out.
9) If one wrote the divine name double, in places where the tradition is to cut out the divine name, it was already discussed. The second name is excised because the first was appropriately written. This is the rule with all double words, that the second is erased. If one erroneously excised the first one, according to the Keset Sofer the writings are permitted.
10) When the divine name must be excised, the divine name is stored in a secure place where it will not be treated inappropriately. It should be stored in a glass jar and not like is done by the minority that it is glued in the doors of the holy ark, for this is not correct at all.
11) To scrape off the divine name[22] is forbidden because there is the fear that the person will ח"ו erase the divine name. Even if the person is an expert and very careful, the person may not rely

[21] The language of the Keset Sofer is: והשם שכותבים בסידורים ב' יודי"ן ווא"ו על גביהן מותר למחוק אם הוא לצורך גדול.
[22] The words are לקלוף את השם and the implication is to scrape away the letters from the parchment, hoping to remove the letters in their entirety.

on his skill כי אין חכמה ואין תבונה ואין עצה לנגד ה' in places where one may come to erase the name of Hashem which is respected and exalted הנכבד והנורא. Sometimes, the ink in absorbed in the parchment and person is cutting into the divine name. If one acted inappropriately and scraped of the divine name, such that the parchment underneath remained, it is forbidden to write another word on that spot, because the divine name acquires its place קנה מקומו and the sanctity permeated from side to side.

12) To excise or to scrape away some of the letters from the divine name or the letters accociated with the divine name הנטפלות and attached to the end פשיטא דאסור is forbidden, because this is comparable to erasing the divine name.
13) The divine name is not written on a [23]מטלית because of the fear that it will separate from the parchment and it will not be treated appropriately ח"ו. Some permit this. In all circumstances one must be meticulous not to write the divine name half on a מטלית and half on the sheet, even in instances which are permitted with other words.
14) The holy name, may not be turned to the mundane. For example, if one had to write ויאמר יעקב אל יוסף אל שדי and he forgot to write the words אל יוסף and he began to write the holy names אל שדי and after he wrote the holy name אל for the holy purpose he realized he had skipped the words אל יוסף, and now the scribe wants to write the word יוסף and the name אֵל will be read as אֶל with a segol, this is forbidden.
15) There was an incident with a scribe who in the verse ויאמר ה' אלקים אל הנחש skipped the divine name אלקים and was not certain if his intention when writing the word אל was for the word אל and the divine name אלקים was completely forgotten or if his intention was to write the divine name and he wrote the two letters אל and he forgot and wrote the word הנחש. It was ruled that it was not proper to erased the word אל, out of concern that it was sanctified. To erase the word הנחש and to complete the divine name was also not proper, since the letters אל may not have been sanctified. Rather the person should excise the word אל and write the holy name anew.
16) We have already written that a name which is not holy may not be sanctified. If one was inappropriate and sanctified the writings, rather intentionally or by accident, the word may not be erased, and it must be excised from the sheet.
17) לכתחלה it is forbidden to write the divine name outside of a ספר so that it will not be mistreated. Therefore, the divine name is not written in letters. There are those who are carful when writing the word שלום not to complete the writings. However, most if the world is not meticulous in this regard.
18) If the divine name was written or inscribed on a vessel, the divine name should be excised and put in גניזה.

[23] As was explained previously, the מטלית is when there is a whole in the parchment and a piece of parchment is attached from the other side. The writings may usually be continued on this attached piece of parchment, which is filling the hole.

12 One who made a mistake when writing the divine name, or if the writing deteriorated the method of their correction
18 sections

1) If one needed to write the divine name, and intended to write יהודה and by mistake did not place a daled in the word, and the divine name is thus written, but it was not sanctified for holy purpose, the divine name is invalid. This name should not be erased, but rather excised.
2) If one was to write יהודה and the intention of the scribe was to write יהודה, but the scribe omitted the daled, the daled can be attached above יתלה הדל"ת למעלה. Now that the tradition is not to hang letters, even with the hung daled the reader might read it as the divine name, after the daled was hung, the heh should be scraped away and then דה should be written and the hanging daled should be scraped away.
3) If the intention was to write the divine name, but it was written in place where יהודה should have been written, it is forbidden to hang the daled (because by writing the hanging daled the scribe is effectively erasing the divine name) and even if the scribe realized immediately after writing י"ה and he wants to complete the word יהודה it is forbidden to do so. Since the letter י"ה can not be erased, even בדיעבד they can not be allowed to remain but rather must be excised.
4) The scribe had to write the divine name, and he sanctified it but accidentally wrote יהודה, he can make the daled into a heh and then erase the last heh. Some say that he must initially make the daled into a heh and then erase the last heh and some say that the order does not matter and he can first erase the last heh and then make the daled into a heh.
5) If it was found in a sefer torah, a place where instead of the divine name was the word יהודה, and it is impossible to clarify from the scribe if the word was sanctified or if it was not sanctified, one should be stringent because of the uncertainty. The method of correction is not to make the daled into a heh, because it is possible the writings were not sanctified by the scribe and the intention was to write the word יהודה, and to erase all of it is not proper because it is proper the scribe intended to sanctify the writings in which case the י"ה can not be erased. Therefore, there is no method of correction. Rather the sheet must be removed or the word must be excised.
6) If it was the opposite, in a place where it should have been written יהודה the divine name הויה, may It be blessed, was found, according to the Kesset Sofer the daled should be inserted hanging, or the heh should be erased and the ד"ה should be inserted. However, if a place where the word should have been יהיה was found the divine name הויה, may It be blessed, according to the Kesset Sofer, one should be stringent.
7) If one accidentally added a letter into the divine name, for example, if in the name הויה the first heh was written twice, the double and the subsequent letters may be erased. As soon as a letter which had no place in the divine name was added, the holiness ceases from there and onwards visa via the prohibition of erasing the divine name. If one added at the beginning of the divine name, for example there were two yuds, the first yud should be erased and the rest should remain in its holiness.
8) If the divine name אדוני was written with an extra vuv, the vuv should be scraped away and the daled should be extended so that it will be close to the nun. This is not a problem of erasing the

divine name since the vuv was not sanctified as far as erasure of the divine name. This vuv was never sanctified since this divine name has only four letters. The same would be if one wrote the name הו"יה with a double vuv, the extra vuv should be scraped away and the first vuv last heh should both be made thicker.

9) Similarly, if a letter from the divine name, there is no sanctity on the subsequent letters. For example, if one forgot the yud of אלקים it is permissible to erase the mem and then write י"ם. Since there is no explanation or association with this mem to the word אלה, and it is less than the נטפלות which come after the divine name. Similarly, if one accidently wrote אלהנו missing the yud, it is permissible to erase the נ"ו and to write ינ"ו. This is because the נ"ו does not have the sanctity of the divine name since there was no complete divine name, since the yud was missing.

10) If the divine name אלה was found missing a vuv, it can not be corrected. The sheet must be put in גניזה or the word must be excised.

11) If one intended to write אלקיכם and the scribe forgot to write the kof and he thus wrote the divine name אלקים, according to the Kesset Sofer it is forbidden to erase the mem and write כ"ם.

12) If the yud of the divine name was found to be larger than appropriate, such that it appears to be a small reish, and the child identifies it as a reish, according to the Kesset Sofer, it is proper to scrape away the yud and write it again. However, at the time of the scraping the person should

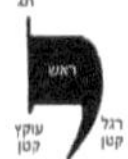

be meticulous that at not time will the letter have the form of the yud. It would be better if it could be corrected with addition of ink, until the letter has the from of the yud and the entire name would retain its holiness. Similarly, if the yud of the divine name was found with עוקץ which is extra long and the child identifies it as a ches, if it can be corrected with the addition of more ink, the ink should be added. If one erases this letter, it must be erased in such a way that at no time is the form that of a yud.

13) If the kof peshuta ך in the divine name אלקיך had an excessively long גג, if the רגל can be elongated until it is twice the length of the גג this is ideal. If this is impossible, the person can scrape away from the גג as written in section 8:9. And one should be careful not to begin scraping from the end of the גג but rather from the part closest to the רגל.

14) If ink dripped on a letter of the divine name, or if the letter became invalidated some other way, such that part of it must be scraped away, or if it is not sufficient to scrape away some of it because it will then be חק תוכות and the entire letter must be scraped away, it is permissible to scrape away or to erase to correct the divine name. This is not the דרך מחיקה, the method of erasure, rather the method of correcting.

15) Similarly, if one letter became attached to another, the space between them can be scraped away (as long as this is not a violation of חק תוכות see sections 8:15 & 8:16). As much as possible a person should be careful to scrape away only the connection and not the actual letter. The person does not need to pass the quill over this divine name t sanctify it.

16) Similarly, if a hole was found on the side of a letter of the divine name, such that it would be invalid. The scribe should scrape away a bit of the letter to make it מוקף גויל surrounded by parchment and then attach a stop gap from the back of the parchment so the hole will not be visible. The bit of the letter which is scraped away is not erasure but rather corrections, because until now it was not kosher and now it is kosher.
17) A heh of the divine name had the limb attached to the גג. If the attachment is thick such that it is recognizable to everyone as a ches, whether this was made at the time of the writings whether this was made subsequently, the רגל may be scraped away and corrected. It was explained in section 8, that the entire רגל must be erased and it is not sufficient to scrape away the connector alone, because of חק תוכות. Therefore, if one began to scrape away the רגל from top ot bottom, as soon as a bit of the רגל was erased the letter will have the from of the heh and it would be forbidden to touch the heh to erase (since a divine name created by חק תוכות is forbidden to be erased). However, as far as the holy writings they are invalid because of חק תוכות. Therefore, the scribe msut be meticulous to scrape away from the bottom to the top and then write it again anew for sake of the sanctity of the divne name. One must be meticulous in this regard each time a letter of the divine name must be erased.
18) If it is not ממש completely attached rather it is slightly attached and it still has the form of a heh, there is a difference. If it was made like this at the time of the writing it can be scraped away in the method previously described. However, if at the time of the writing it was separate and then it became slightly attached since it was the divine name it is kosher. Now that it still appears as a heh, it is uncertain whether or not it can be scraped away.

13 The measurements of the Sefer Torah and the measure of the pages and lines
8 sections

1) The sefer torah should not have a girth greater than its height and not a height greater than its girth. This means that the intention should be that a string which encompasses the entire sefer torah should be the same measure as the wideth of the sefer torah. This is the mitzvah of beautifying mitzvahs זה אלי ואנוהו. If it would be excessively long or excessively thick it it will not be so beautiful. What is the width? By גויל it should be six handbreadths טפחים just like the size of the לוחות. This is twenty-four fingerbreadths using the width of a normal finger which is the measure of seven normal hairs, one tightly adjacent to the other, והן באורך שתי שעורות בריות. By קלף it should be more or less the girth as the height. Similarly, if a person made a sefer torah on גויל which was less than six handbreadths and he minimized the script, or he made it larger than six handbreadths and enlarged the writings, he has done as commanded. And the עמוד שבתוך בספר some say is part of the measurement of the width and it must be medium and ome say it is not part of the calculation, and the latter view is prevelant.
2) The length of each שיטה line is thirty letters, such that the word למשפחותיכם can be written three times. The line should not be shorter so that the sheet does not appear to be a letter. The line should not be excessively long, so that the eye will have trouble finding the beginning of the next line. This is specifically by כתיבה דקה but by כתיבה גסה all is dependent on what is most beautiful and the eyes will not wonder since the writing is large. This is the tradition.
3) Regarding the number of lines in each column the tradition is not to have less than forty-eight, analogous to the travels of the Jews, and some say not less than forty-two וסימן ה' ב"ם סיני בקודש. There should not be more than sixty lines, corresponding with the sixty-ten thousand Jews. The beginning of holiness is forty-eight or forty two and continues until sixty. If one changed these number they did not invalidate the writings. The tradition is to scratch below an extra line, on which there are no writings. This not מעכב.[24]
4) A יריעה of parchment should should not have less than three דפין (columns) and not more than eight. If one had a sheet of parchment with nine columns, the sheet should not be divided such that it will have three columns on one sheet and six on the other, rather it should be split such t there are four columns on one sheet and five on the second. The most beautiful is considered when there are between four and five columns. This applies to all the sheets of the sefer torah except for the last. At the end of the sefer torah, even for one verse it has its own columns and it is stitched with the other pieces of parchment. Even though the last verse does not have words to correspond with the number of lines, the letters should be made long, from top to bottom so that one letter takes up four or five lines, so that the writings will be concluded at the bottom of the column. If there are many verses, the scribe can write on each line one word, to correspond with the number of lines. This is because there is no other solution.
5) When one concludes the writing of the torah scroll, they must finish the writings in the middle of the line at the end of the column so that all will know this is the concluding verse of the sefer torah. This would not be the case if the entire line was used. If the writings were concluded at

[24] i.e. This last line does not invalidate the writings one way or the other.

the end of the line some say the sefer torah is not valid, and some permit, and the עיקר is to permit the use of this torah scroll.

www.ingramcontent.com/pod-product-compliance
Ingram Content Group UK Ltd.
Pitfield, Milton Keynes, MK11 3LW, UK
UKHW041924190726
13854UKWH00003B/1438